SCHOOL
TURNAROUNDS

SCHOOL TURNAROUNDS

The Essential Role of Districts

HEATHER ZAVADSKY

Harvard Education Press
Cambridge, Massachusetts

Second Printing, 2015

Copyright © 2012 by the President and Fellows of Harvard College

Library of Congress Control Number 2011941947

Paperback ISBN 978-1-61250-134-5
Library Edition ISBN 978-1-61250-135-2

Published by Harvard Education Press,
an imprint of the Harvard Education Publishing Group

Harvard Education Press
8 Story Street
Cambridge, MA 02138

Cover Design: Sarah Henderson
Cover Photo: Blue Mountain Images/Getty Images

The typefaces used in this book are Legacy Serif ITC and Knockout.

THE EDUCATIONAL INNOVATIONS SERIES

The Educational Innovations series explores a wide range of current school reform efforts. Individual volumes examine entrepreneurial efforts and unorthodox approaches, highlighting reforms that have met with success and strategies that have attracted widespread attention. The series aims to disrupt the status quo and inject new ideas into contemporary education debates.

Series edited by Frederick M. Hess

Other books in this series:

The Strategic Management of Charter Schools
by Peter Frumkin, Bruno V. Manno, and Nell Edgington

Customized Schooling
Edited by Frederick M. Hess and Bruno V. Manno

Bringing School Reform to Scale
by Heather Zavadsky

What Next?
Edited by Mary Cullinane and Frederick M. Hess

Between Public and Private
Edited by Katrina E. Bulkley, Jeffrey R. Henig, and Henry M. Levin

Stretching the School Dollar
Edited by Frederick M. Hess and Eric Osberg

CONTENTS

FOREWORD

ix

INTRODUCTION

1

CHAPTER 1

*The Context of School Reform
and Turnaround*

5

CHAPTER 2

*The Role of Districts in Reform
and Turnaround*

19

CHAPTER 3

Charlotte-Mecklenburg Schools

55

CHAPTER 4

School District of Philadelphia

81

CHAPTER 5

Denver Public Schools

113

CHAPTER 6

Sacramento City Unified School District

141

CHAPTER 7

Long Beach Unified School District

165

CHAPTER 8

*Comparing Approaches:
External-Partner-Led, District-Led,
and Charter Partners*

187

CHAPTER 9

Learning from Turnarounds

203

NOTES

229

ACKNOWLEDGMENTS

235

ABOUT THE AUTHOR

237

INDEX

239

FOREWORD

Back in the day, we thought that the school was the center of change and that reform would take place "one school at a time." The school-based reform movement of the early 1990s was led by the development of whole school models supported by the privately funded New American Schools Development Corporation. Models such as America's Choice, Success for All, and Expeditionary Learning remain today as successful examples of how to improve student achievement by organizing schools around common research-based practices, materials, and organizational structures. In the subsequent wave of school-based reform, charter management organizations (CMOs) such as Achievement First, KIPP, and Green Dot were able to develop even more robust models by utilizing the vehicle of state charter school legislation. Charter school models were able to improve student learning through variables such as time and teacher quality by transcending industrial-style collective bargaining contracts and school district bureaucracies.

Several decades later, experience suggests that while individual schools are indeed the center of change, the improvement of low-performing schools cannot be implemented at scale or sustained without redesign of the larger system in which they reside—the school district. We now know that school redesign, replacement, and repurposing and new school development (all encompassed by the widely used term *turnaround*) are in fact the work of effective school districts and that school districts improve by creating the capacity to turn around their lowest-performing schools.

The late Peter Drucker said that "every organization is perfectly designed to get the results it is getting." Nowhere is this as true as in the relationship between a school district and the schools it operates. To change school results, we have to change the design of the school. That requires a district that redefines itself around the capacity to systematically create a portfolio of higher-performing schools. It requires a change in almost every aspect of the traditional American school district—from systems for accountability, resource allocation, and talent development to methods of assessment, instruction, intervention, and operations. It also suggests that all schools in the portfolio offered by a district to its public may not be district operated. A *diverse provider strategy* embraces external operators and partners, applies accountability, and grants autonomy on the basis of achievement regardless of who operates the school. It is through this redefinition of the school district that the full range and capability of school turnaround models can be realized.

There is a growing consensus among leading urban school districts across the country that turning around the lowest-performing schools is the *primary* work of districts. School turnaround is distinguished as a key element of the Portfolio School District movement that has been defined through the intellectual leadership of Paul Hill and the Center for Reinventing Public Education, which now includes a network of over twenty major cities in the United States. Turnaround in this district reform model is the vehicle by which the quality of a district's portfolio of schools is improved.

In 2009, the U.S. Department of Education attempted to stimulate school turnaround through $3.5 billion in School Improvement Grants (SIG). However, if the experience of its predecessor, Comprehensive School Reform (CSR) Program, is anything to judge by, it is doubtful that the turnaround measures implemented in the SIG schools will be sustained beyond this grant's three-year funding cycle without the commitment of the districts in which they reside to improve, replace, and turn around their chronically failing schools on a long-term basis. No good or bad school exists in isolation in its district. In fact, most of the decisions that determine whether or not the school remains low performing or improves lie outside of the school and reside with district leadership and governance. After all, if the school could improve to an acceptable level on its own it would have already done so.

Turning around low-performing schools requires more than commitment and good intentions on the part of superintendents and boards of education. It requires a theory of action; new policies, systems, structures, procedures, supports, interventions, and designs; and different ways of doing business. Sustaining "new" schools requires the alignment and institutionalization of new systems in a coherent plan. In this important book, Heather Zavadsky looks at the successful efforts of five districts to close the achievement gap by stimulating the improvement of their lowest-performing schools and describes the way they went about this messy and often contentious work. She chronicles the challenges and successes of the Charlotte-Mecklenburg Schools, School District of

Philadelphia, Denver Public Schools, Sacramento City Unified School District, and Long Beach Unified School District in turning around their lowest-performing schools in different political, structural, and social contexts.

Through the leadership of their superintendents, these five districts made a commitment to enable all of their students to attend a good school. They developed a strategy to do it, learned from their experiences, and made adjustments along the way. The districts discussed in this book created a path to school turnaround in the context of their own culture and community. Some of their ideas, methods, and approaches are transportable, while others can be modified and applied differently. Most importantly, their experiences with scale, as described by Zavadsky, can inform this important work for other school districts.

Inspired by some of the same methods and systems detailed in this book, my former school district of Hartford, Connecticut, replaced or redesigned its lowest-performing schools over a period of five years to create a portfolio of higher-performing schools. After four consecutive years of significant gains in student achievement and a doubling of the graduation rate, Hartford rose from the lowest-performing district in the state to the most improved. While this transformation has been subject to extensive analysis and interpretation, I can tell you that it occurred simply and fundamentally by enabling more students to attend more good schools.

As this book is published, the future of school turnarounds is at an important junction. If more school districts do not follow the examples of the five mentioned in this book, states will find it necessary to accelerate involvement and assume the control necessary to improve failing schools. The recent experience of the Recovery School District in New Orleans suggests that a portfolio of schools operated exclusively by a variety of charter school networks and other external providers within the parameters of a state accountability plan can effectively replace the traditional school district model.

School Turnarounds is a great sequel to Laura Pappano's *Inside School Turnarounds* (Harvard Education Press, 2010) and significantly expands on the early turnaround work of Cincinnati and Hartford.

Heather Zavadsky captures in clear, concise language the many complex systems and structures five leading districts developed to turn around their lowest-performing schools while providing a road map that others can follow for the critical work of improving low-performing schools. She provides inspiration to superintendents, principals, teachers, school board members, and policy makers in the form of proof points that support the essential premise of this book: school turnaround, while difficult, is indeed possible, and should be the primary work of school districts.

Steven J. Adamowski
Special Master
Connecticut State Board of Education

INTRODUCTION

In 2001, Turner High school* was not a place parents flocked to for their children. It was dark and chaotic, and student performance was abysmal. Less than 30 percent of the entering ninth graders would graduate, according to longitudinal achievement data.[1] Teachers came to school at the same time as the students, lunch extended over two hours and was unruly, shootings were not unheard-of, and the school had maintained the lowest academic standing in the state—*academic emergency*—for several years. Now fast-forward to 2010, where Turner has earned the highest rating in the state—*excellent.* How did that happen?

Turner's turnaround effort was implemented within its existing structure, because it took place before *turnaround* became the formalized policy it is today. The change was made by replacing the principal, but not the staff, which does not match any of the four approved models under the current SIG policy. The new principal worked to rebuild relationships within the school and the community, set firm expectations that everyone opted to "take rather than leave," he garnered numerous

---

* A pseudonym.

resources and support from local business. With the addition of just a few leaders and teachers he brought in, Turner was transformed into a "high-tech" high school, using virtually the same staff. The first two to three years saw huge cosmetic changes (thanks to a lot of paint, elbow grease, and volunteers), positive cultural and climate changes, but little change in achievement. However, academic success began to move around year three.

This is the type of successful turnaround story one likes to hear; particularly with the amount of money currently invested in turning around schools. But what happens to Turner if the talented principal who worked relentlessly to move the needle leaves, or if the school loses supports because it is off the failing school list? What if other students want to attend a school similar to Turner New Technology High School? Is this a model that can be picked up and replicated as an answer for chronically low-performing schools? Can it be sustained once created? Would the transformation have occurred under the new federal policy, with its mandated improvement trajectory of three years, rather than the nine-plus years that it actually took?

This book provides the opportunity to consider the above questions and the impact of the School Improvement Grant (SIG) through the lens of five urban districts that are implementing innovative and systemwide turnaround strategies to improve chronically failing schools. The purpose of the book is to show how turnaround is being implemented in practice in very different contexts. Rather than boil down dramatic school improvement into a portable set of best practices, it aims to illustrate, within the five case studies, how complex systems are addressing the essential elements of school improvement: effective human capital strategies, rigorous and engaging instruction, continuous performance management, positive cultures of high expectations, collective accountability, immediate and targeted interventions, and strong connections with families and communities, among others. In addition to these practices, the case studies will illustrate how different organizational structures, models, and partnerships interact with variables such as size, union contracts, and state policy both successfully and unsuccessfully.

The districts in the book each have their own unique features and challenges that make for interesting and informative case studies on scaling turnaround or school improvement at the district level. For example:

- Charlotte-Mecklenburg Schools recently won the 2011 Broad Prize for Urban Education, and is implementing extremely innovative and forward-thinking human capital strategies.
- The School District of Philadelphia has targeted ninety-five turnaround schools and is doing well despite the recent (and unrelated) resignation of the superintendent and two board members and conflicts with the teacher's union.
- Denver Public Schools is implementing two large regional turnaround strategies that include a number of schools that co-share buildings with charter management organizations.
- Sacramento City Unified School District is using a data inquiry process to deeply examine and improve instruction in collaborative teams.
- Long Beach Unified School District exemplifies a stable and high-functioning system that has not had any schools in corrective action for several years.

Whether this book is about *turnaround* as defined by the U.S. Department of Education through the models and approaches required in the SIG program, or about coherent systemwide school improvement depends on the interpretation of the districts in the book and by the reader. Because these districts are implementing most or all of their strategies districtwide, the distinction of the two interpretations becomes blurred. Therefore, the term *turnaround* in this book is used interchangeably with *school improvement*.

The initial selection of these districts was based on their application of a districtwide turnaround strategy and student achievement scores. Additionally, I attempted to include districts that used varying levels of external assistance. For example, Denver developed its own School Turnaround Office and then engaged the assistance of an external partner the next year. Philadelphia managed its own turnaround strategy, which included charter-led schools. Because selection was based on set criteria, this study is qualitative and uses case study format to capture how the realities of culture, politics and funding enable different individuals in different systems to change the educational trajectory for students systemwide.

1

⌘

THE CONTEXT OF SCHOOL
REFORM AND TURNAROUND

While writing this book, I've been challenged by the term
turnaround. Likely this is because it represents a "re-
packaging" of education reform work that has been in exis-
tence for many years and increased with the release of the semi-
nal report *A Nation at Risk*. The report sounded the alarm about
the number of subpar schools educating our nation's children.
Fueled by the idea that the right approach—or model, or funding, or people—can remedy a large number of schools, we continue a relentless pursuit of a better way to educate all kids.

We have been trying to improve schools for years. The closer
we look, the more we learn. We readjust our targets and goals,
create a new movement, learn some more, and so on. Before
A Nation at Risk was released, we focused on literacy, fueled by
books like *Why Johnny Can't Read*.[1] After some flirting with
open schools and other approaches, we eventually shifted our
attention to student outcomes in the early 1990s through *outcome-based education*. Then we began understanding that we

wanted more than just certain kids to achieve high outcomes, so we shifted our efforts to schools and their application of coherent research-based instructional methods through the Comprehensive School Reform (CSR) movement. While our focus on school improvement gained some success in schools here and there, it seemed to happen too slowly and only in particular schools. With the passing of No Child Left Behind in 2002, it became obvious which schools and children were falling through the cracks.

NCLB is an influential and sweeping educational policy that set an important, and what I believe to be improved, reform approach. While there are many problems with certain aspects of the policy, it has helped us refine instructional strategies for different students by more clearly defining (although at the state level) what is to be taught and better identifying who did not master which strategies and objectives.

NCLB also continued to set a bar of acceptable performance (again at the state level), outlined in the Title I Act created under the Elementary and Secondary Education Act (ESEA) and impose sanctions for those not meeting standards. A school failing to make Adequate Yearly Progress for four years would be in *corrective action*: in the fifth, it would enter *planning for restructuring*; and in the sixth year, it would be required to implement one of the five proposed models under NCLB:

- Close and reopen as charter
- Contract with private management company
- Replace all or most staff
- State management
- Other major governance restructuring that makes fundamental reforms

Between 2006 and 2007, the majority of the schools had selected the "other" category and used supported teams as their most common tool. When 2009 American Recovery and Reinvestment Act funds became available through the School Improvement Grant (SIG) program, the unprecedented funding prompted districts to go back and better structure their plans for chronically failing schools. The reform landscape gained a new term of art: *turnaround*. The turnaround model is one of four models for prescriptive intervention in the SIG. But for many, and for the purposes of this book, the term *turnaround* refers generally to the difficult work of improving chronically failing schools.

As with all education legislation, the SIG has some aspects that are questioned by practitioners and researchers, but it also has many aspects that incorporate and build on important lessons learned from previous reform efforts. The remainder of this chapter will outline the SIG grant, dive deeper into previous school-led reform movements, and introduce the thesis of the book: how districts can and should be leveraged for taking turnaround to scale.

THE FEDERAL ROLE IN TURNAROUND

In August 2009, U.S. Secretary of Education Arne Duncan announced that an unprecedented amount of funding—$3.5 billion in Title I School Improvement Grants (SIG)—would be invested in the nation's lowest-performing schools. This huge influx of resources was intended to provide states and school districts with the means to increase graduation rates, reduce dropout rates, and improve teacher quality for students. Additionally, the DOE designated $4.35 billion in competitive Race to the Top funding and $650 million in Investing in Innovation (i3) funds. The largest chunk of turnaround money falls under the SIG program to support rapid improvement in the "persistently lowest-achieving schools" through four prescriptive intervention models:

- *Turnaround*: The local education agency (LEA) replaces the principal and rehires no more than 50 percent of the staff, gives the new principal greater autonomy, and implements other prescribed and recommended strategies.
- *Restart*: The LEA converts or closes and reopens a school under a charter school operator, charter management organization, or education management organization.
- *School closure*: The LEA closes the school and enrolls the students in higher-achieving schools in the LEA.
- *Transformation*: The LEA replaces the principal (except in specified situations), implements a rigorous staff evaluation and development system, institutes comprehensive instructional reform, increases learning time and applies community-oriented school strategies, and provides greater operational flexibility and support for the school.[2]

The tight structure of the four prescriptive models is just one area where turnaround policy has become much more rigid. States are also given strict guidelines on how to distribute SIG funds to the lowest-performing schools. Priority is given to Tier I and II schools (described next) that have not met adequate yearly progress under Title I for at least two years. Thus, states are to select schools by determining the number of low-performing schools, the tiers the schools fall under, and the LEA's capacity to implement the prescriptive models and strategies in the SIG program. The tiers are defined in general as follows:

- *Tier I*: Title I schools that failed to make AYP for two-plus years and are in "improvement," "corrective action," or "restructuring" and are identified by the state education agency (SEA) as the lowest-achieving 5 percent of those schools in the state, or as a high school with a graduation rate below 60 percent for a number of years.
- *Tier II*: Secondary schools that are eligible for, but do not receive, Title I–Part A funds and are identified by the SEA as "persistently lowest-achieving."
- *Tier III*: Schools eligible for Title I funds, improvement, corrective action, or restructuring that are not Tier I schools.

Priority for SIG funds goes to Tier I and Tier II schools, and the schools must use one of the four models. Once those schools are served, Tier III schools may be awarded grant money, and those schools do not have to use one of the four models. According to a May 2011 DOE baseline analysis of SIG applications, among the fifty states and Washington, DC, 16 percent of all schools are eligible for SIG funds, 86 percent are Tier III schools, and 7 percent are Tier I and Tier II schools.[3]

CRITICISMS OF SIG

After several years of SIG implementation, there has been significant pushback on several aspects of the program, including perception of a lack of flexibility and practicality behind the models, concern about inconsistent state-level implementation, and questions about clear expectations from the program. According to Rob Manwaring, the rigid format of the SIG program was in response to a lack of progress in earlier turnaround attempts through the CSR Demonstration Program.[4] According to a West Ed report, schools under that program had complete flexibility, which in many cases lead to inaction (more on this next).[5] The SIG program represents the U.S. Department of Education's (DOE) attempt to provide the right amount of guidance and flexibility.

Some of the main criticisms of the SIG program are about the four prescribed models. Researchers and practitioners assert that the models were built on a weak evidence base and fail to provide flexibility where needed. A report by the California Collaborative on District Reform (CCDR), which partners with the American Institutes of Research (AIR), provides some interesting critiques of the four models that are worth consideration.[6] One of the main points is that these models do not leave much flexibility to adapt to context. For example, each model requires removal of the principal, suggesting that the principal is the source of the problem in chronically low-performing schools. While many practitioners agree the principal is a key factor in school performance, some can cite examples where that is not the case. Additionally, the CCDR report suggests that removing 50 percent of the teachers in the turnaround model is an arbitrarily set figure—why not 25 percent or 60 percent? Finally, it points out that districts with more than nine schools falling under the federal definition of chronically low-performing are allowed to select the transformation model for only half of the schools identified for intervention.

Superintendents and turnaround leaders also contend that the models are too restrictive. Most district leaders interviewed in the CCDR study voiced a preference for designing their school improvement approaches around the particular needs of each school and its community. One superintendent referred to four models as attempting to cure something unique like cancer with a "standard cocktail." He explained, "It's not like treating the same disease; each person has different DNA. Each school and community is unique." Another found the prescriptive nature of the SIG program to be problematic because "not every school in improvement needs the same thing. They need a customized solution." Other leaders voiced concern about the number of requirements in the transformation model because, "it reads like a checklist of fifteen things; they end up not doing any of them well." A superintendent of a large urban district insisted that flexibility was necessary to allow different types of innovative school models to meet parent and school needs. She felt the focus needed to move away from the "adults in the system" and should center on creating unique programs.

Several practitioners thought the models were acceptable, particularly if the models provided more flexibility. They also felt the timeline created the necessary urgency to begin work on chronically failing schools, but that academic changes might not be visible until after several years of implementation. Two leaders said they felt there was not clarity in the SIG program as to what defined "success," meaning how much improvement was expected with the funds. Overall, most appreciated the focus on and funding for struggling schools. However, two superintendents stressed that although the SIG program was an issue worthy of high focus, particularly if viewed as a supplement, it was not a replacement for good district-level reform strategies.

In 2010, U.S. Senate and House of Representatives education hearings urged Congress to incorporate more flexibility within turnaround policy. The recommendation was in response to schools' feedback that the proposed models unfairly laid all the blame for underperformance on school personnel and were too restrictive.[7] Additionally, the models required actions that were not always possible or feasible for schools to employ. For example, schools implementing the transformation model are required to increase student learning time, implement a "rigorous" teacher evaluation, and show great operational flexibility. Yet implementing these practices is extremely difficult at the school level, particularly in schools where union contracts restrict practices such as the number of hours teachers can work, or in rural schools, where resources can be scarce. One way the DOE has worked to address such challenges is to provide technical assistance and other forms of support to schools in turnaround. For example, the DOE held a SIG conference for schools serving rural and Native American students, to learn more about their challenges, provide suggestions, and create a network between schools with similar challenges.[8]

In reality, few schools have had enough time to show dramatic changes, and results from these interventions have been mixed.[9] However, many schools that received SIG grants are in their second year of implementation and are seeing positive results from the approaches they designed. Other than the pushback around lack of flexibility, the main problem researchers and practitioners are finding with these interventions is that they fail to acknowledge the importance of the district's role in supporting and preventing chronically low-performing schools.

TURNAROUND TO DATE

When I am visiting with practitioners and policymakers across the country about school turnaround, it becomes apparent that I am not the only person unclear about what it means to be "in turnaround." To practitioners, it typically means a set of schools that have been chronically low-performing and are working to improve. At the federal level, the meaning is much more specific and revolves around the SIG program; it is a policy designed to improve the nation's schools that are in the bottom 5 percent according to academic achievement. A report summarizing the SIG applications from all states and Washington, DC, shows that despite the DOE's attempts at tight implementation through the four prescriptive models, SEAs still brought wide variation in how they executed and managed their grants, including how they selected schools and how they supported and monitored progress. For example, 8 states monitored their schools monthly, 9 quarterly, 1 twice per year, and 33 annually. Even the definition of *monitoring* varied. Thirty-nine states conducted site visits, 16 planned "check-in" meetings, and 16 used online tools and data systems to monitor progress. Regarding administration, SEAs were allowed 5 percent of their grant to fund administration, evaluation, and technical assistance to schools. Examples of how states chose to use these funds include the following: 26 states chose to enhance their system of support to target schools, 12 planned to reorganize or create a new office to support SIG schools, 18 developed quality control measures for external providers, 10 developed or mandated

13

school/district improvement tools, and five engaged the assistance of higher education institutions.[10]

School-Level Reform

It seems surprising that school reform efforts often call for research-based interventions, when the research base on the success of school-level reform itself is so thin. Take the CSR program: in 2001, Congress appropriated $235 million to support the reform of two thousand schools. The premise was that this movement differed from past efforts in its application of comprehensive practices intended to strengthen all aspects of school operations: curriculum, instruction, professional development, parental involvement, and school organization.[11] But the key findings from WestEd's five-year evaluation of the program was that it did not yield widespread achievement gains or make comprehensive changes in its selected schools. While the evaluators did find a few schools that made some measureable achievement gains, those gains were achieved through very different approaches that were highly contextualized. Additionally, schools that did not have the knowledge or resources to improve those areas of their operations were not able to improve student performance.

The evaluators concluded that there is no single method for improving schools, except that the successful schools did a better job of connecting and aligning activities that resulted in achievement gains. Interestingly, case studies in this report comparing CSR schools and non-CSR schools in the same district found similar aligned practices in CSR and non-CSR schools. For example, the evaluators found the same data-use and teacher planning practices across all schools in the same districts. These schools also showed similar achievement growth, suggesting that their districts had a positive influence on implementing intended practices that the CSR policy attempted to require.

In a separate study of the CSR schools that showed dramatic improvement in a short amount of time, respondents in about half of the schools cited district support, guidance, and assistance as being instrumental to their success.[12] Another study, showing slightly different conclusions, found that CSR schools that implemented programs with high levels of fidelity over three to five years did yield statistically significant increases in student achievement in math and reading. This report hypothesized that the prescriptive nature of one commonly implemented model, Success for All, was found in several of those schools.[13] Nevertheless, these studies all agreed to some extent that the CSR movement did not yield widespread improvements in student achievement hinged on full program implementation; and had some utility in its emphasis on systemic reform approaches, particularly when approached from the district level.

District as Turnaround Lever

The authors of the CSR evaluation cited fragmented application of the elements of the CSR model as one of the main reasons for the project's lackluster results. Consider how things might have turned out differently if, for example, fifteen of those two thousand schools were in the same district, and that district was able to train and support those schools in implementing strong practices in curriculum alignment, strategic human capital strategies, instructional programs and interventions, and performance management. Is this something that the district could appropriately do for each school, despite variations in context, instead of leaving them to figure the work out on their own, or find the right research-based approaches to apply?

There has always been a debate in school reform work between district centralization and decentralization. Do we need to let schools that represent a microcosm of their own unique community make all the decisions to suit their own needs, or do we trust districts to coordinate the distribution of resources and make certain decisions, such as selecting curriculum programs, to create alignment across schools? We have all read about schools that, like the few cases mentioned in the CSR evaluation, are "beating the odds," heroic principals who "clean house" and shift their culture, and charter schools that are making remarkable academic improvements. The problem with those examples is that their reform efforts can easily unravel without district support, such as succession planning to ensure that the school always has effective leaders and teachers or curriculum alignment to ensure that students from each elementary school are well prepared when they move up to middle school.

There is a growing body of evidence that suggests that districts and central office can play a key role in improving struggling schools while ensuring that their other schools continue to perform well and avoid future need for drastic intervention. In their study of five well-improving high-poverty districts, Togneri and Anderson assert that the districts they studied were successful due to their shift from a fragmented operational focus to building a common vision and then an infrastructure to support the vision.[14] As I found in my extensive study of five Broad Prize winners, the central office is a logical catalyst for building commitment and alignment systemwide.[15] Each district was well aware of who in its schools was struggling, and had a plan to provide supports and interventions.

Chapter 2 details the important role of districts in school reform and potentially in school turnaround. Researchers and practitioners agree that districts represent a crucial element of turnaround work. Robert Hughes, president of New Visions, has said, "Turnaround efforts won't succeed if they are only school-focused and are not complemented by system change . . . No bad school is an island; it exists in a system."[16]

2

THE ROLE OF DISTRICTS
IN REFORM AND TURNAROUND

Chapter 1 discussed implications of one of the largest investments in school-level turnaround, the Comprehensive School Reform (CSR) movement. While the evidence from one large study showed that the CSR program itself did not yield expected results, it did find several schools that made noteworthy improvements. What's interesting is that some of those improved schools were non-CSR schools, which makes attributing the successes to the CSR program alone problematic.[1] The authors suggested that the more successful schools appeared to have better systems and alignment in place, with the source of the system often coming from the district rather than schools.

This finding comes as no surprise, and agrees with what I saw in my years coordinating and studying districts that were finalists and winners of the prestigious Broad Prize for Urban Education.[2] The Broad Prize provides a good set of exemplar districts to study because of the years of data and interview information behind the process. Having empirical performance evidence is important for ensuring that valid examples are identified and accurate descriptions are used. The Broad Prize selection process has proved to be effective; when conducting site visits, I found that districts that withstood the massive data examination to become one of five (now four) finalists out of one hundred eligible districts (now seventy-five) each year also proved to have well-aligned systems and strategic approaches to their reform paths. Many of these districts also showed the ability to sustain their noteworthy achievement gains, further evidence of coherent systems that made these districts' reform approach a part of their culture rather than an add-on program or grant. For example, Boston was a finalist for four consecutive years, and then a winner in 2006. Long Beach (California) won the Prize in 2003, sat out for the required three years after winning, and then reemerged as a finalist in 2007, 2008, and 2009. Many other finalists continue to be repeat finalists over time, like Charlotte-Mecklenburg (North Carolina), Miami, Broward County (Florida), and Socorro (Texas).

In *Bringing School Reform to Scale* ("*Reform to Scale*") my study of five past winners (which were also repeat finalists)—Aldine (Texas), Boston, Long Beach, Garden Grove (California), and Norfolk (Virginia)—I found that these districts had very different characteristics and contexts, but they also had a surprising number of system similarities. These are also found in current Broad Prize winners and districts that are receiving other awards and recognitions.[3] These common characteristics agree with findings from education reform research by reputable researchers like Elmore and Ferguson on the critical components needed to make meaningful change that can translate into better teaching and learning in classrooms. Education reform, whether it is a movement like turnaround, an innovative program like T-STEM, or just considered school improvement, still must address the instructional core and the management systems around the instructional core. This chapter discusses the necessary elements to improve and support the instructional core, explains how they can be applied to turning around chronically low-performing schools, and highlights areas where policy can help create the conditions to support those practices.

SYSTEMIC REFORM

School reform has been a topic of urgent concern for decades, and it remains at the forefront of policy and practice, often prompted by particular historical events or major policies, including the launching of *Sputnik*, the Civil Rights movement, pivotal reports like *A Nation at Risk*, and policy movements like Goals 2000 and No Child Left Behind. While our nation clearly still has underperforming schools and segments of the student population who are struggling, we have also gained some agreement about the educational improvement process from an array of research and practice.

What we agree on by and large is that there are several important elements in school improvement that are also interconnected, specifically: clarity on what is taught and learned; the right talent to deliver and lead instruction; an array of appropriate instructional programs; continuous data and monitoring systems; a menu of interventions to address performance concerns; and sensitivity to contextual realities, such as school and community culture, parent involvement, governance, and resource allocation.[4] Not only are these pieces important, but they are also relevant even to what seems like minor and isolated program tweaks. If the school (or district) decides to push Algebra I down to eighth grade to better prepare students for math, leaders still need to consider what math skills are taught prior to eighth grade, how to clearly articulate the new scope and sequence, who is trained to teach eighth-grade algebra, what program will actually be selected, and if there is a particular instructional approach that should be used. Having data to show if students understand the foundational concepts in the correct sequence is also important, as is their mastery of the course content. The school will also need a set of interventions to address remediation for struggling students. All of these pieces need to be in place for the course to be effective and need to be developed within the context of existing policy, resources, and relationships.

In addition to connecting and leveraging these instructional pieces, it is also important to think strategically about the school improvement process. One of the biggest problems cited in reform literature is the common reactionary approach of layering on programs that become Band-Aids rather than long-term strategies to well-defined goals. In his book *Spinning Wheels*, Hess talks about the danger of schools and districts jumping to adopt the latest and greatest program without giving much thought to how a particular program will address instructional goals and how it will fit within the larger instructional program.[5] If a program does not yield expected results immediately, schools often drop that approach and start another, sometimes in place of the previous program, or on top of existing programs. What this stopping and starting regime does is create a culture of "this, too, shall pass," and it can open up the system for instructional decision making driven by special interests or politics rather than desired results. The outcome is a patched-together educational program that feels as fragmented to students as it does teachers and leaders.

One important commonality shared by many of the Broad Prize districts is their understanding that scaling improvement beyond one great teacher or school requires aligning the parts of the system around core elements linking directly to teaching and learning.[6] How to link those pieces within a thoughtful, aligned, and strategic reform framework is a recurring theme in this book. While the CSR movement in the 1990s attempted to address a similar holistic improvement approach, it missed the idea that many aspects of these practices are best coordinated and supported by and with the district central office, and then between schools, classrooms, and teachers. In this book, I contend that focusing turnaround on single schools will have far less impact and sustainability than a district applying a more systemic and strategic approach.

Next is an explanation of how several Broad Prize districts systemically approached school improvement in the areas proven to be crucial to turning around chronically stuck schools: leadership and human capital strategies, instruction, culture and climate, stakeholder engagement, and an overall understanding of how to differentiate, monitor, and intervene to meet the needs of the entire system. *Reform to Scale* provided far more detail in each area; this chapter aims to provide some examples of important practices to consider in systemic reform and how these practices apply to the current turnaround movement. I would typically address curriculum first because that is where most districts begin their reform work, clearly defining what is to be taught and learned.

23

However, this chapter addresses staffing practices first, because it is this area that most closely ties to turnaround and has many policy and practice elements that cannot be employed without district support.

HUMAN CAPITAL STRATEGIES

Education is a human-intensive endeavor. Turning around chronically failing schools requires leaders and teachers with specific skills and talent that not everyone possesses. Curriculum, performance management, interventions, and stakeholder engagement all impact the instructional process, of course, but talent management is the one area turnaround hinges on, and thus it is one of the most important pieces to get right. Good leaders and teachers can mitigate the problems that come with a poorly aligned curriculum or lack of data—but this cannot be done if such people are not in place.

The intense focus over the past five years on leaders and teachers has built an understanding that talent management involves much more than just recruiting, selecting, developing, and retaining talent. It means understanding how to obtain and distribute the right leaders and teachers, and then lining up all parts of the system to help them successfully meet their goals. This comprehensive approach also considers human resources (HR) practices like compensation and benefits, tenure, and succession planning and instructional support practices like having time to meet, instructional coaches, user-friendly data systems, and a well-aligned curriculum.

The importance of talent management is one area in which policy and practitioners tend to agree; it takes unique skills to turn around, close, restart, or transform chronically failing schools. Many actions associated with attracting and supporting individuals with those unique skills happen well beyond the school level. School boards (and sometimes city leaders) and a district's reputation attract superintendents, and superintendents attract, vet, and place principals. Additionally, the district serves as the first tier for recruiting and hiring teachers and develops policies and practices that affect leaders and teachers. At the school level, principal leadership and support play a large role in bringing in and keeping effective teachers. These connected activities shared between the district and school levels have a huge impact on ensuring the presence of uniquely talented leaders and teachers; one of the areas where the district's role in turnaround is most apparent and extremely important.

Leadership

Almost every research study or article on turnaround points to leaders as the main catalyst for changing what happens in chronically low-performing schools. This is because principals have the ability to lead the vision, set expectations, build the right culture and climate, and improve student learning by engaging teachers, staff, parents, students, and the community.[7] Although principals are a crucial factor, they are selected, supported, and directed by policy and practice driven by the district superintendent, who is responsible for orchestrating districtwide turnaround approaches. The Broad districts profiled in *Reform to Scale* and the case studies featured in this book had strong, forward-thinking superintendents who were able to lead achievement improvement across classrooms and schools.

Aldine's former superintendent Nadine Kujawa, who came up through the district ranks in over thirty years of service, set up and operationalized the belief that poor children can do better than "just survive." She believed it was up to the adults in the system to be clear on what students were to know, and to get them there by whatever means necessary. However, she also knew that it was up to the leaders in the district to provide tools to manage and monitor the process and to ensure that appropriate supports were deployed in a timely manner. Kujawa helped build collective accountability in the district so that everyone was engaged in activating that belief, and the data showed that the district's vigilant focus on student performance and system alignment made "educating every child in the district" more than just nice words in a belief statement.

Tom Payzant came to Boston Public Schools as the third superintendent in five years. He brought focus and stability into a district mired in politics, racial unrest, white flight, and poor performance. From inside the system, Payzant worked to set clear expectations about student learning and focused on instruction, leadership, performance management, and relationships. From outside of the system, he made sure he attended and joined meetings with the school community, businesses, parents, and the teachers' union.

Like Payzant, Laura Schwalm brought focus and alignment to Garden Grove, along with the persistent refining of practices through continuous performance monitoring. She set a climate and culture that expected students to go to college and supported the adults in the system to help them be successful. She balanced goals and aspirations by focusing on short-term goals to encourage personnel with "quick wins," as well as long-term goals that took steady focus, patience, and a close eye on performance.

Long Beach has been fortunate to have two powerful, steady superintendents over the last twenty years: Carl Cohen from 1992 to 2002, and then Chris Steinhauser, who came in in 2002 and continues to hold the position at the time of this writing. What developed from their leadership became known as *the Long Beach way*, exemplified by expectations around specific instructional strategies, a focus on college readiness, and constant adjustments based on their continuous data monitoring. The Long Beach way means being clear on goals and expectations and not joining movements simply because they are recommended, but rather using data to make decisions. Long Beach successfully avoided having any of its schools identified on the state's list of lowest performers—the district is highlighted in chapter 7 of this book as an instructive example of prevention.

When John Simpson came to Norfolk in 1998, he said student performance was "abysmal." He recentralized many district practices, raised expectations, changed and aligned the curriculum, and sent a strong message about student and staff expectations. As one district leader described it: "You could feel a change in the seriousness of purpose with the work, and you could feel a change in strength of leadership. You could really feel it as clearly as you could feel the wind blow. This was a new day, a consistent message that was committed and passionate, highlighting what was possible."

When he spoke of the district's efforts Simpson always said "we" rather than "I," and the district displayed a culture of high expectations and the desire to examine the "brutal facts" from the perspective of "What do you need?" and "How can we fix this?" rather than blame.

Leadership stability is a major factor in school reform. Much has been written about the tension between the three to five years it takes to make and sustain reform and the fact that the typical superintendent term is three years or fewer. While those numbers anecdotally seem to be improving in some large urban districts (where turnover is typically the highest), 2011–12 seems to have seen more superintendents retire or leave to work in the private sector. Whether this is due to a higher number of leaders reaching retirement age or the difficult climate created through unusually large budget constraints, the loss is serious, since leader stability is key to reform. The five districts in *Reform to Scale* had superintendents who served no fewer than six years; Tom Payzant served the longest—for eleven years. Long Beach and Garden Grove still have same leadership as when the book was written in late 2009. Aldine's leadership switched while the book was being written, but saw very little shift in its reform approach. Boston and Norfolk now have completely new leadership, with Norfolk on its second leader since the book was written. The *Reform to Scale* districts, as well as several cases discussed in later chapters in this book, did well in leadership succession planning at the school level and in distributing leadership throughout the system so that reform approach(es) did not rest within one individual. In Garden Grove, Laura Schwalm created a strong, very small central office cabinet with seven key leaders who knew each other's jobs so well they could step in to help each other at any point. When Peter Gorman announced that he would be leaving Charlotte-Mecklenburg in June 2011, the school board asked that he help select potential candidates who could keep their reform work on track.

Clearly, hiring a new superintendent is one of the most important roles of any school board. How a school board approaches replacing a superintendent is crucial, particularly when the board and the district constituents believe the exiting superintendent had a good plan in place that showed evidence of working. One thing a board should keep in mind is how common it is for new superintendents to unravel a system that is working because they feel the pressure or need to put their own "footprint" on the district by using their own approach (which likely was applied in a very different context). If the board feels most or all of what is in place is working, it might behoove them to seek an individual who is comfortable continuing to support that work and who will make refinements based on facts and data.

Building a pipeline of school leaders is also incredibly important, and was done in different and creative ways in the *Reform to Scale* districts. To develop internal talent, Boston instituted the Leadership Institute and the Boston Principal Fellowship; the latter involves a year-long residency with participants "living the life of a principal" for approximately eighty-five days. Norfolk sent interested future principals to a program supported by a local business consortium called the Center for Creative Leadership. Whether an internal or external candidate, principals in the five *Reform to Scale* districts all had numerous opportunities to meet with colleagues and gain targeted professional development, and many had mentors who were retired principals. Long Beach used an innovative model to create both support and alignment across principals of different levels by having co-principals work together in high schools. The two principals would have equal roles; with the added twist that one often came from the elementary or middle school level. Another effective professional development approach employed for principals was to train them in new instructional techniques with teachers or before teachers received training to ensure that they knew how to observe and support teachers who were implementing new instructional programs.

Teachers

Having an ample supply of effective teachers is also important. Many of the Broad Prize districts also have internal development programs for teachers. One of the most well-known and successful of those programs is the Boston Teachers Residency (BTR), created in 2003 to counteract heavy teacher turnover and to recruit more high-need teachers like math, science, and teachers of color. The BTR is a thirteen-month training program that follows a medical residency model and puts its candidates in the field on a weekly basis to work side by side with experienced teachers. In addition to working directly in classrooms four days a week, the residents receive training on Boston Public Schools' culture, curriculum, and unique instructional techniques through the yearlong placement in a "successful" classroom. This key element of the program is important for BPS, as this information cannot be provided through higher education academic training programs. BPS's instructional programs are difficult to implement and require dedicated training and practice. Once the program is completed, candidates earn a master's degree, teaching license, and a forgiveness loan of $10,000 for tuition. The ability to directly award participants with teacher certification is an integral part of the program, made possible by the district's partnership with the Massachusetts State Board of Education.

The other important component of hiring in the Broad Prize districts was that teachers and sometimes leaders were asked to participate in rigorous performance-based interviews. For teachers, this often meant teaching a sample lesson or responding to various scenarios. For principals, it meant having their past achievement scrutinized and responding to "in-basket" (a simulation of the various types of activities that would fall onto a principal's desk, ranging from replacing a teacher to responding to an irate parent) exercises and various scenarios. Leaders and teachers were carefully selected and matched to the needs of schools and classrooms, according to the data gleaned and the characteristics of the school community.

Training and Support

The keys to professional development for both leaders and teachers in the *Reform to Scale* districts was for it to be relevant, accessible, accountable by use of follow-up activities, and aligned to school and district goals. When questions about professional development are asked in a poor-to-average district or school, personnel point to a thick notebook of offerings from which teachers can select. In a good system, professional development activities are selected based on data, contain follow-up support and expectations that new learning will be found on lesson plans, and meet the needs of individual teachers. Teachers cite good professional development as a retention tool; they value the training they receive and feel that it improves their instruction.

Another important source of support cited by teachers in the *Reform to Scale* districts was other teachers. Teachers highly valued having structured weekly time to meet with each other to review data, plan lessons, and share materials. The most productive teacher meetings were held regularly and were structured with a skilled facilitator, an agenda, and respectful full participation. In those districts, I witnessed several very productive teacher meetings where teachers had open, honest conversations about student-level data, how they did on specific instructional strands, and which teachers the group should look toward for the best instructional strategies on specific topics.

Teachers also appreciated having the support of instructional coaches, a resource that many leaders cited as having the most instructional "bang for the buck." This model appeared to be particularly popular with teachers because it was easily accessible within their own classroom, and was done is a meaningful way either through codeveloping lessons, coteaching, or receiving helpful feedback from a respected master teacher. Boston had a more formalized coaching model, Collaborative Coaching, which involved several steps to give teachers ample opportunity to work with coaches. A different and creative version of the coaching model was found in Norfolk, where the central office merged its curriculum and development division with its professional development division to create the Leadership and Capacity Development Department (LCD). Personnel in the LCD department spent 70 percent of their time working directly in schools with teachers and principals to ensure that curriculum and instruction were being implemented well. Teachers in Norfolk often asserted that their LCD specialists were an important source for helping them address tricky instructional issues.

Human Resources Practices

Central office human resources (HR) departments represent the public face of personnel recruitment and application and set the procedures for vetting and getting potential leaders and teachers through the door. Central office and schools, to varying degrees, share creation and implementation of policies and practices around salary and benefits, professional development, and evaluation, and set the culture for schools and classrooms. The *Reform to Scale* districts made changes in their HR practices that improved their ability to hire effective leaders and teachers. Some of those changes were simple, like improving (or in Boston's case, just creating!) Internet application processes, making hiring timelines earlier so that schools could more easily compete for the "best" teachers, attracting and vetting the right candidates through the use of Web-based tools like the Gallup Perceiver (which assesses instructional knowledge, for example), and better defining the type of candidate the district is seeking, as Garden Grove did in its latest teacher recruitment brochures.

A more complex view is to consider HR as part of a larger approach to ensuring the district has adequate leaders and well-supported teachers. System talent management entails having the HR department work more closely with other departments like curriculum and instruction and professional development to ensure each piece is working together. Some connections between these areas have been achieved through increasingly popular "pay-for-performance" or "strategic compensation programs," which provide additional dollars to teachers and sometimes leaders who yield better-than-average academic gains over the course of a year. Because strategic compensation done well requires connection between payroll, HR, professional development, data, interventions, and various other departments, these programs are often driven from the superintendent's office rather than HR, since top-level administration is more able to easily connect with and impact those areas. The advantage of keeping all instructional-related divisions connected to HR is similar to what Norfolk accomplished by merging their curriculum and professional development departments—better alignment to match talent with system needs.

This section only touched on promising talent management practices, which are extremely relevant for turnaround work. Strong leaders are needed for turnaround to set focused goals and align practices and supports with those goals in a very strategic and focused manner. The most successful turnaround schools have had clear focus, concise and consistent messages, aligned supports, and leaders and teachers who are able to address whatever was missing or not working instructionally to help students succeed. Schools are not equipped for strategic human capital management to the same degree as districts. Because of this, districts are much better positioned to ensure that struggling schools are provided with a strategic approach, a strong leader, effective teachers, and supports to line up all the parts to make marked changes to the instructional core.

CURRICULUM AND INSTRUCTION

What is taught in schools is almost as important as who manages and supports instruction. Concern that our nation is not preparing students well for college or to function and compete in a workforce requiring different skills has strengthened our desire to better define what should be taught and learned. Two proofs of this growing interest are the number of states engaged in defining common national standards and the concern over the number of remedial courses students must take upon entrance into college. While agreeing as a nation what American students need to know and be able to do has thus far proved to be a herculean task, for the most part many states are working toward better defining what preparation for college and skilled careers looks like. Not only is it important to decide what skills students should have acquired upon exiting the K–12 system, we then must align the K–12 instructional pipeline to achieve those outcomes. Although many Broad Prize districts started building their curriculum on their state standards, they were careful to closely review them through data and consult with teachers to ensure each grade progressed without any unnecessary repeats or gaps in the instructional sequence. Much of that work was coordinated by both winners and finalists through the district office, along with teachers and leaders and sometimes external curriculum experts. Aldine started its curriculum revision process in 1997 and has been refining the curriculum ever since. To address its new instructional goals and programs, Norfolk updated its curriculum to ensure that students were able to master the state standards and beyond. The end result was that teachers in these and other districts felt that students were coming to them from previous grades better prepared, student achievement was increasing while achievement gaps were reducing, and students were able to handle more advanced classes and apply to and attend college.

The curriculum is the backbone of instruction, and how it is developed and who is involved is almost as important as the content. If the curriculum is handed down from on high by a district or an external expert hired by the district, it may fail to get buy-in from school personnel or fail to meet the needs of schools. However, if teachers develop curriculum at the school level, they end up spending valuable time out of the classroom. Additionally, curriculum set at the school level is not conducive for student mobility or for grade-level alignment, which is why many of the Broad Prize districts facilitated the curriculum development and revision process by involving central office curriculum directors and specialists, representative samples of teachers, and external experts as needed. With involvement at all system levels, other tools and practices—such as program selection and supporting tools like curriculum guides and/or a Web-based interface connecting to lesson plans and data—can contribute to this process.

Curriculum plays a crucial role in school turnaround. The extent to which a school has a rigorous, aligned, and clearly communicated curriculum has a direct impact on teaching and learning. Curriculum can ensure that each subject-area scope and sequence will correctly build instructional concepts, adequately prepare students for grade-level transitions, and clarify whether teachers understand what is to be taught. While most might think these elements already exist within schools, they do not—not because schools are not doing a good job, but primarily because it is difficult work that takes time, close monitoring, proper measurement systems, and tight collaboration across what are often large and diverse systems. The district plays an important role in setting curriculum, because it has the ability to convene the right set of people to develop and refine the curriculum and can ensure that curriculum and instruction are equally rigorous across all schools. Just as curriculum alignment across grades ensures that cross-grade transitions are seamless, instructional alignment across schools is equally important to ensure that student education is not disrupted if that student moves across town or that it is of lesser or better quality depending on zip code. While there do not appear to be any formalized studies comparing curriculum alignment and turnaround, there are some that hint, and I can attest anecdotally, that districts with clarity around what is to be taught in every school have a lower rate of schools in need of turnaround, particularly at the upper grades.

INSTRUCTIONAL PROGRAMS AND PRACTICES

Curriculum and *instruction* are terms that can be easily confused and are often used interchangeably. I tend to think of curriculum as the scope and sequence in different subject areas that are built upon state standards, while instruction defines *how* the curriculum is to be delivered. In *Reform to Scale*, I detailed how the districts selected instructional programs and explained how several districts employed particular instructional approaches—such as Aldine's use of Bloom's Taxonomy to identify the cognitive level of each lesson or Norfolk's *Instructional Non-Negotiables*, a set of principles employed around instruction like using data, functioning like a learning community, and planning instruction collaboratively. Long Beach uses a similar set of instructional principles called the Essential Elements of Effective Instruction. One of the most important instructional practices revealed by the Broad Prize districts was how instructional programs were selected, monitored, and evaluated, and how the system prepared students if the district decided to ramp up instruction to higher levels.

The important theme found in program selection in these districts was the agreement that practices around program selection are far more important than the programs themselves. In other words, a district should not adopt Saxon Math because many people say that it is a great program. A district should select its math program according to data needs, review the success of that program through formative data, and should cease using the program if the data show the program is not meeting desired results. Boston selected programs by using a committee composed of leaders and teachers to develop a detailed rubric on the type of program desired and then identify specific requirements (such as having supplemental work for advanced students) and desired implementation effects. The committee would review several programs using the rubric, select the top three, and then pick one or all three to pilot with a few students. If the program yielded positive outcomes, then the district met again to consider larger or full-scale implementation.

One aspect of program selection has seen improvement in Texas, prompted by the current budget crunch, districts are more closely evaluating their programs to ensure they are effectively educating a sufficient number of students. A recent conversation with the chief finance officer in Aldine revealed that the district has been evaluating its programs over the past few years to cut out any programs that were not maximizing educational opportunities for a large enough subset of students. For example, a reading program was discontinued several years ago because, while it did increase reading scores for students, it intervened with only a handful of students. It was replaced with a program that was anticipated to yield similar results but for more than twice as many students.

Raising overall instructional rigor was another common practice in the *Reform to Scale* districts. Garden Grove spent several years eliminating as many remedial courses as possible to provide more grade-level courses for students. To ensure that struggling students could still succeed, the district worked with teachers on remediating students' skill gaps and offered several options for interventions, like double-block classes that serve

38

as an hour of preview/review before the actual grade-level class, which is scheduled for the next hour. Additionally, districts worked to ensure that students were put in the right courses—courses that would challenge them and help prepare them for college. Long Beach and Garden Grove worked together to give their teachers Advanced Placement (AP) instructional training and focused on preparing more students with additional bridge-builder classes for the advanced rigor of AP classes.

To change or improve the instructional core, schools and districts should have a clear understanding about what they believe high-quality instruction looks like and how it's delivered. In Garden Grove, such improvement means ramping up instruction throughout all grade levels to prepare students for college. In Aldine, it means focusing on Bloom's Taxonomy. In Norfolk and Long Beach, it means having Instructional Non-Negotiables or following the Essential Elements of Effective Instruction that define a process around the teaching and learning cycle using data and learning communities. Schools in turnaround need to be clear about instructional approaches, particularly across grades and schools. Just as aligned curriculum helps with grade and school transitions, so, too, do well-defined and aligned instructional strategies.

DATA USE, MONITORING, AND PERFORMANCE MANAGEMENT

To determine that the right leaders and teachers are in the right place and have timely supports, that the curriculum is properly aligned, and that all students are successful (as defined by the district) requires the ability to continuously monitor all parts of the system. While it seems straightforward that performance management means the presence of data, there are some important considerations for building the proper tools, practices, and culture to make data useful. There must be a user-friendly interface where users can easily obtain numerous types of data on students and schools, time to review data in collaborative groups, an understanding of how to interpret and react to data, structured monitoring systems (like walk-throughs), a system to tie data points together to assess progress on district and school goals, and a culture and climate of trust that is comfortable with and eager to use data as a flash-light rather than a hammer. Collapsing those practices into four essential categories, it takes (1) powerful data management systems, (2) various data collection tools, (3) an accountability tool to manage all the data pieces, and (4) a culture of trust that values data.

Data is an important driver for improving district practices that will result in increased student achievement. The *Reform to Scale* districts all showed a commitment to collecting and using data to inform individual, classroom, school, and district instructional decisions. The best data systems are those that allow users to review formative and summative assessment data; see student record information like transcripts, absences, and discipline data; and connect to the curriculum or standards. While all *Reform to Scale* districts had comprehensive data management systems, Boston had one of the most sophisticated systems, which closely tied numerous data sources to instruction. MyBPS was developed for Boston in 2003 as a means for making data useful to administrators and teachers. The secure Web-based system contains formative and summative student assessment data, student record data, tips on how to use and interpret the data, links to state standards and learning objectives tied to assessment questions, and samples of exemplary student writing compositions and scores. Interactive graphs displaying student performance data linked to specific questions on state assessments are also available.

Constantly monitoring if students are mastering learning objectives was another important common practice in the *Reform to Scale* districts. Teachers in Aldine gave students common and benchmark assessments anywhere from every three to six weeks to ensure students were mastering learning objectives and to regroup and match students (even at the elementary level) to teachers based on student needs and teacher strengths. To examine and react to data collaboratively, teachers in the *Reform to Scale* districts reviewed formative assessment data together and adjusted instruction accordingly. If one teacher did a good job in a particular learning objective, the other teachers would work with that teacher on developing a re-teach unit, and would then use her lesson plan and support for that objective in subsequent years. Teacher team meetings were open and often looked at teacher-level data together to problem solve and plan instruction. Teachers in these districts felt this constant collaborative scrutiny of student learning was important both for monitoring curriculum alignment and for ensuring that instructional issues were addressed immediately, avoiding the need for more intensive interventions down the road. The frequent monitoring appeared to pay off—teachers and leaders in the *Reform to Scale* districts often would say "there are no surprises" because of their constant monitoring of student success throughout the year.

In addition to assessment data, the *Reform to Scale* districts monitored classroom instruction through structured walk-through processes. The walk-throughs differed from typical classroom observations and were done to monitor instruction and identify support needs. Significantly, most of the districts kept their walk-throughs separate from teacher evaluation. The structured walk-through process often entailed having a team composed of leaders and teachers who would use a rubric to document specific target practices or activities, such as using appropriate questioning techniques. John Simpson in Norfolk explained that it was important at first to keep walk-throughs separate from evaluation and confidential so that teachers would view them as supportive rather than punitive. Eventually, Norfolk teachers wanted to share their walk-through results with leaders and other teachers.

With the growing number of online tools that add ease to data collection, it is not difficult for systems to become overwhelmed with data, becoming "data rich" but "information poor." Even though various data points are important for targeting support and resource needs, it is important that districts understand why they are collecting data and have an organized way to review and respond to data. The *Reform to Scale* districts each had an overarching tool for monitoring district and school performance and then tying that data to district and school goals. The tools were reviewed at least quarterly and often included both summative and formative data, as well as walk-through observations and in some cases qualitative data. Aldine uses a Baldrige-based scorecard that includes formative, summative, and walk-through results that directly feed into action plans. Scorecards have been implemented at the classroom, grade, feeder-pattern, and district levels. Boston's Whole School Improvement Plan includes formative and summative assessment data tied to school goals that feed into the district's goals. Garden Grove monitors school performance through the Single School Plan, which utilizes formative and summative data along with data from Action Walks to measure progress toward school and district goals. Norfolk's Comprehensive Accountability Plan includes three tiers that contain summative and formative performance data as well as a narrative that analyzes the different data points within the schools' context.

Results from these data systems are often found on district intranets and posted on walls in schools and district offices. The transparency of data and the conversations around data speak to the open and trusting climate created to make the data about improving student achievement rather than finger-pointing at the adults in the system. While trust is a fuzzier thing to measure, it is quite obvious when it has been permeated throughout a district. Conversations throughout the *Reform to Scale* districts always were around data and often characterized as being an interesting problem to solve. I heard statements like "We looked at the data and wondered *what was going on* with that one set of fourth-graders" or "We looked at the data and just didn't get it right, so we worked together to find a better way." Teachers seemed comfortable saying, "Wow, that lesson really bombed, so I went back to the drawing board and worked with another teacher to build a re-teach lesson." Administrators took particular care when introducing new practices and approached these tasks by empathizing with the common unease new practices create and providing support along the way. When teachers in Garden Grove were first asked to give quarterly assessments, they were naturally nervous. Laura Schwalm described their approach as "building out a platform from a cliff." She explained, "It's new and scary, and they want to back up and say, 'We can't go here, the kids will fail.' So you hold them, build out the platform further, help them get closer to the edge, and tell them, 'It'll be okay, we'll help you.' Sometimes you still go too fast, and you push them over the edge. So you apologize, dust them off, and bring them back up. It's all about timing, but it's been effective and we've listened along the way and made adjustments as needed."

This trust has been important to move the system forward and to encourage teachers and leaders to take risks. It has also helped put the focus on students, because the adults in the system know that they'll be supported.

Turnaround cannot happen without data, because data is the pathway to prevention and appropriate intervention. Chronically low-performing schools will not improve without the presence of easily accessible data, strong monitoring systems, an overall strategy for benchmarking multiple data points against district and school goals and targets, and a positive and trusting climate that views data as a tool to improve instruction for students. Behind every school that has seen turnaround success are teachers and leaders who have been using strong data and accountability tools and practices to improve instructional decision making.

INTERVENTION AND ADJUSTMENT

The other key to making use of data is to have an array of interventions available to meet the unique needs of students, teachers, and leaders. It is also helpful to have a method for solving problems and identifying which interventions to apply. Several of the *Reform to Scale* districts used various means for solving problems. Aldine followed a structured problem-solving process called a *root cause analysis*: (1) collect data, (2) chart potential causal factors, (3) identify the root problem, and (4) recommend an intervention. Struggling schools in the *Reform to Scale* districts received ample support and attention from central office leaders and were often identified as *focus schools*, a technique that is common in turnaround approaches. Interventions in the focus schools were varied and ranged from adding on instructional coaches to providing more aligned professional development and even applying hard or soft reconstitutions.

The biggest lesson on interventions from the *Reform to Scale* districts was the importance of using prevention as an intervention. In other words, the districts and schools used their continuous data and monitoring tools to identify problems that were easy to mitigate within the regular school day and classroom, rather than waiting until more intensive interventions were needed. Additionally, prevention also meant intervening in earlier grades, like preK, so that students started school with the necessary skills to succeed. Instructional techniques that were also useful for intervention were helping teachers learn to better differentiate instruction for students and to use flexible student grouping. In Garden Grove and Long Beach in particular, prevention meant focusing on appropriate classroom placement for students in order to prepare them for college; for example, Garden Grove leaders focused on better informing teachers and counselors how to identify students for acceleration (as Schwalm said, it's not always just the quiet kids that sit in the front of the room). Students who were identified as gifted but chose not to participate were flagged for later advanced courses.

Students displaying more pervasive instructional issues were provided a number of options, with the focus on keeping remediation efforts within the instructional day rather than before or after school. Individual intervention plans for students were mentioned in several of the districts, and all districts discussed addressing student intervention with a collaborative team approach. For students not passing benchmarks or state assessments, before- and after-school programs and tutoring were available, and some students were retained in particular grades to master content before transitioning to the next grade.

The challenge with interventions is that they become more difficult to align seamlessly with a student's regular instructional program the further away they get from the regular school day. To eliminate instructional fragmentation, tutors were required to work closely with teachers to make certain that the additional time was used well and benefited the student. Teachers implementing any intervention were well supported by intervention teams and through targeted professional development. Interviews with teachers confirmed that they saw a reduction in the need for intensive interventions outside of school as a result of students coming to them better prepared than in previous years, when their systems were not as well defined or aligned.

Turnaround in of itself is an intervention, and typically one that addresses situations that have become so serious that it would be extremely difficult to put things back on track. It is important that districts understand how to intervene with struggling schools, even if it means the district must first learn how to do so through an external partner, which will be discussed in chapter 8. Second, it is important that districts have a range of interventions in their toolkits to address the unique needs of students, teachers, and leaders. The best intervention is prevention and is provided immediately and within the school day. Focusing on keeping students on track is one of the best ways to avoid the need for more intensive interventions like school turnaround.

INFLUENCING FACTORS

The work of schools and districts does not exist within a vacuum. Even districts that have the right personnel, instruction, data and monitoring, and interventions in place can fail if other relationships are out of balance. For example, while Long Beach has maintained improvements in student achievement, there was a two-year period during which the district thought this achievement would unravel due to issues arising between the district and the teachers' union. Stakeholder relationships are very important so that districts have the ability to implement what is needed for school improvement. The districts in *Reform to Scale* had positive relationships with their school boards, teachers' union or association, parents, and the community. The leaders in these districts made sure that they had the right people at the table to make decisions and gain information, and they made it a point to communicate frequently with various stakeholder groups. Interviews with community members in Boston revealed that Tom Payzant frequently attended various community meetings to learn about issues and concerns that could affect the school district. In Aldine, the district and community worked together to rebuild a dilapidated apartment complex into a new elementary school.

One of the most important relationships in districts and schools is with parents. Because low parent involvement is a common concern with chronically failing schools, reconnecting parents to schools is crucial. The districts in *Reform to Scale* engaged parents with many forms of communication and in many different languages. If parents were not comfortable going to the school, school personnel went to parents. One way these districts increased parent involvement was by making engagement more meaningful for parents. Rather than having parents come in to make photocopies, the schools had them share information about their jobs with students or read to them. The schools were flexible so that parents could come to events at the school at various times of the day, and they offered different types of classes to parents, such as parenting, English, or computer classes. The *Reform to Scale* districts viewed their schools as an extension of the community, and often opened their buildings for community events or meetings.

THE ROLE OF POLICY

The U.S. Department of Education, state and district departments of education, school boards, mayors, and other governing agents all play a role in school reform. While there is not always clarity on what policy can and cannot do, the general belief is that it can incentivize practices, support practices, stay out of the way, or hinder practices. As I mentioned in chapter 1, I believe NCLB and SIG have helped education in many ways by providing at least some level of focus on standards, disaggregated data, and accountability. SIG in particular has generated urgency and set a timeline for addressing our lowest-performing schools and it has incentivized schools to take bolder and more innovative actions. However, some recommendations laid out in SIG conflict with or are not supported by other state and local policies and conditions that can either support or block large-scale changes across districts. For example, practitioners in this study and/or in my state often cite several factors that affect their ability to follow the requirements found in SIG. They include the following issues.

Transformation Model. The requirement to develop teacher and school leader effectiveness is impacted by several issues:

- This strategy requires the use of student growth to improve teacher performance. However, some states, like Texas, do not have a student/teacher link, making implementation of this practice difficult. Additionally, states with a strong union presence receive major pushback implementing this policy.
- Identifying and rewarding school leaders and teachers can be difficult in states and districts that do not have a nuanced enough evaluation tool to differentiate teacher performance. Additionally, many states, like Texas, lost funding or do not support performance compensation programs.
- Policies affecting teacher licensure, alterative pathways to teaching and/or principalship, and teacher preparation in universities can have an effect on the pool of qualified and trained teacher or principal candidates.
- Teacher union contracts greatly limit a district's ability to select and place teachers in its schools. This has been a particularly damaging practice when seniority rules result in the layoff of large numbers of new teachers who have been specifically recruited, placed, and trained in schools applying any of the four SIG models.

- Contracts that limit the amount of time teachers spend in school can also impede coordination of important instructional tools, such as having common planning time for teachers to meet and scheduling professional development.

Turnaround Model. The requirement to replace at least 50 percent of the staff as required by the turnaround model can be difficult to execute under restrictive union contracts. State laws, limited data, and/or union contracts can affect the ability of a school to use appropriate evaluation systems to identify which teachers to replace. In addition, teacher contracts often impact a school's ability to extend school hours or the school year, which also then limits the district's ability to provide schools operating flexibility.

Restart Model. The ability for a district to partner with a charter management organization (CMO) or an educational management organization (EMO) can be restricted by a state's charter laws or union contract. Charter laws can affect the number of new charters allowed to operate within a state, making funding facilities particularly difficult. Union contracts that do not allow charter school teachers to be members can also impact a district's ability to implement the restart model.

Data and Accountability Systems. States and districts that do not provide longitudinal or student-level data, or do not provide it in a timely manner, greatly impact the ability to focus interventions for struggling students, teachers, or schools, affecting the application of all four SIG models.

School Boards. Some school boards do not support partnerships with charter schools, alternative compensation models, and/or evaluations that tie to student achievement, or they are divided with each other or the superintendent regarding a coherent school improvement plan. One way boards can provide stability and support to the turnaround or school improvement process is the support for keeping effective superintendents in place and replacing superintendents who leave with leaders who will support the parts of the reform that prove to be working.

CONCLUSION

Turnaround work needs to consider the role of the districts attached to chronically low-performing schools. In addition to employing a systemic, customized focus, the district must support several key areas crucial for addressing areas of concern in schools: setting culture, providing a rigorous and aligned curriculum, developing and deploying strong leaders and teachers, using data to make decisions and manage performance, and fostering appropriate internal and external stakeholder relationships to support and sustain improvement, change, and innovation. None of these things by themselves can change what likely resulted in years of poor performance. Rather, the combination and alignment of these areas applied in a strategic, purposeful manner is what research points to as successful for creating and sustaining long-term improvements.

There are examples of districts, turnaround organizations, and even states approaching turnaround work at the district level. Charlotte-Mecklenburg is seeing marked improvements in its twenty lowest-performing schools through a districtwide turnaround approach that involves assessing the needs of each school, providing attention and supports based on those needs, and ensuring that each school has an effective leader and teachers through its Strategic Staffing Initiative.[8] In California, through the California Collaborative on District Reform, eight districts are designing systemic approaches to improve their lowest-performing schools by focusing on district culture, leadership, teaching and instruction, continuous data use, and collaboration with the community.[9]

The five districts featured in this book provide interesting and instructive examples of how districts should be leveraged in turnaround work. While their approaches vary, they share many commonalities, and each had an area of particular strength or uniqueness. Charlotte-Mecklenburg serves as a strong example of a far-reaching and coherent human capital strategy. Philadelphia implemented a large-scale effort using various models and very effective parent and community engagement practices. Denver implemented a regional approach and had interesting examples of how to partner with charter schools. Sacramento reorganized their district's entire infrastructure and approached instructional improvement through an in-depth data inquiry approach. Finally, Long Beach represents a long-standing, high-functioning organization that provides a good example of coherence and prevention.

In the Turner High School example in the introduction, the principal who got his school "unstuck" was hand-selected by a forward-thinking superintendent who approached chronically failing schools in his district holistically, by: implementing budget processes based on student needs; employing a district-wide focus on teaching and learning; providing systemic supports to teachers; implementing a college- and career-ready curriculum; and creating a culture of continuous improvement. In other words, his district was considering turnaround in terms of the entire district system. The aim was to improve the lowest-performing schools, as well as ensuring that performance in current schools did not slide.

Turning around chronically low-performing schools is important work. The Obama administration has stated its goal of improving the five thousand poorest-performing schools in the nation. The half-billion dollar investment in that work has reaped some incremental improvements for pockets of students. However, many of us who have extensively studied school reform know that without the support of the district, these successes likely will not be sustained, and more schools will join the list just as quickly as others earn their way off it. Focus, alignment, performance management, and talent management are crucial for ensuring students can move seamlessly from grade to grade, school to school. For more students to receive ample preparation for their choice of postsecondary experiences, we cannot rely on fixing one school at a time.

The purpose of this book is to show how research on successful district-level reform can be applied in turning around chronically low-performing schools. Through research and interviews with key practitioners, external turnaround providers, and reformers, this book describes the role of the district in improving chronically low-performing schools to scale and creating the conditions to avoid future need for extensive turnaround efforts. Using examples directly from the field, chapters 3 through 7 describe how five districts applied different district-level turnaround approaches to improve their bottom-performing schools. Chapter 8 examines the differences between district-led and external provider-led turnaround efforts, noting the impact of each approach on governance, leadership, partnerships with external organizations, relationships and trust, sustainability, and resources. Finally, chapter 9 summarizes the common themes across the turnaround districts and practitioner perspectives in relation to expectations outlined in the SIG program and concludes with suggestions for practitioners.

3

CHARLOTTE-MECKLENBURG SCHOOLS

Noteworthy practice area: Human capital. Implementing an innovative, strategic, talent management strategy in turnaround schools and across the district.

Chapter Highlights

- Employs an extensive and well-aligned human capital strategy to drive its turnaround approach.
- Places strong leaders and teachers in high-need schools.
- Uses succession planning to ensure that strong leaders are in place in both central office and schools.
- Provides leaders with freedom and flexibility within an accountability framework.

BACKGROUND

Charlotte-Mecklenburg Schools (CMS), located in North Carolina, has been a finalist for the Broad Prize for Urban Education for multiple years, including 2004, 2010, and 2011, when it won the Prize. According to 2010 data, the district has over 133,000 students, 176 schools, and almost 9,000 teachers.[1] This relatively large urban district is also quite diverse: 41 percent of its students are African American, 16 percent Hispanic, 34 percent White, 5 percent Asian/Pacific Islander, and 4 percent Native American/multiracial. A little over half of the student population (51 percent) is eligible for free and reduced-price school lunch, and 12 percent of students are designated as English language learners. The district was led by Peter Gorman from 2006 to June 2011, when he left to work in the private sector.

When I conducted the Broad Prize site visit in 2004, the district displayed a lot of well-aligned, promising practices. It had a good leader, James Pughsley (2002–2005), who was doing well despite the racial tension arising from race-based student assignment to schools. After 2004, CMS dropped off the radar for The Broad Prize and did not resurface again until 2010. The district showed a performance decline between 2005 and 2007, which may have been at least partially attributable to changes made in the state regarding the treatment of special education assessments. After Pughsley left in 2005, the district received some unsavory attention from state judge Howard Manning, who accused the district of committing, "academic genocide" against at-risk low-income students in four low-performing high schools.[2] When Peter Gorman came into the district in 2006, he inherited a large district steeped in negativity, a community that wanted to divide the district to reduce its size, and poor academic achievement in a number of schools. After studying performance across the district, Gorman found pockets of high improvement in some schools but uneven student performance overall. Roughly one-third (165) of CMS schools had significantly lower performance than the rest of the district. In response, Gorman assembled a team to further examine those schools and developed what they and others refer to as a *district-led* turnaround approach.

56

TURNAROUND STRATEGY

Gorman and his team talk about chronically low-performing schools as being "stuck" in a cycle of failure: performance declines, expectations for students drop, families with a choice leave the school, the remaining students have growing needs, resources no longer match those needs, and leaders and teachers do not have the skills or resources to address those needs.[3] According to CMS leaders, stopping that cycle requires:

- Better leaders and teachers with proven track records
- Removal of those who don't support the reform (referred to as *toxic people*)
- A team approach—no lone wolves
- Freedom and flexibility with accountability
- Differential compensation to acknowledge that not all jobs are equal in difficulty

Achievement Zone

CMS began its turnaround strategy in the 2007–08 school year with the formulation of the Achievement Zone (AZ), funded by Title 1 philanthropic funds, and SIG funds. The AZ created six geographic areas that would function as professional learning communities (PLCs) and receive direct oversight and support from the district central office. The AZ was overseen by an area superintendent and consisted of eleven schools. Limiting the number of AZ schools allowed the one dedicated area superintendent, who would typically have overseen more than twenty schools, to focus attention just on the few schools of highest need. In addition, the AZ schools were supported by the "best" central office staff in areas such as transportation, human resources, and finance. The schools also received quick responses

57

from central office when they requested any kind of help and were seen as a priority for services.

AZ schools were selected by performance; some were in corrective action, and many were the lowest-performing schools in North Carolina. The idea around the AZ was that schools would move out as they improved, and new ones would move in if needed. To ensure that other schools' performance did not drop, the district identified additional schools not meeting accountability targets and called those FOCUS (Finding Opportunities; Creating Unparalleled Success) schools. These sixty-five low-performing schools also received additional supplies and materials to improve achievement.

To create a professional learning community among the AZ schools, the AZ principals met monthly with the area superintendent who oversaw them. Each meeting was held within an AZ school so that the principals could observe and conduct walk-throughs for various learning purposes. In the meetings, the principals talked constantly about best practices and existing challenges within their schools.

The central office leader, Curtis Carroll, who led the AZ when it first originated, revealed some other interesting steps the district took to ensure success of the AZ program and CMS schools in general. To change the public's perception, the district hired a community relations specialist to publish positive stories about the schools. In 2008, there were 162 positive news stories about CMS and the AZ schools. "I know the exact number," the leader stated. "With Pete (Gorman), you had to measure everything, and if you were going to meet with him, you needed to know the numbers because he definitely was going to ask for them."

In addition to creating positive press, the district also worked hard to attract more teachers to apply in the district. At a job fair in 2008, Gorman stood outside and shook the hands of over two thousand attendants to personally encourage them to consider teaching in an AZ school. Another important area of focus was safety. Principals worked closely on improving school safety and on creating transparency about the number of arrests and suspensions in AZ schools. The fourth major focus was literacy, which entailed hiring the best English teachers.

Many schools within the AZ showed improved performance after the first year and in subsequent years. However, Gorman did not believe that the AZ should be the only turnaround strategy, because it would not necessarily result in moving strong leaders and teachers into the neediest schools. Thus, he and district staff worked to develop an initiative that would focus more on human capital: the Strategic Staffing Initiative (SSI, described next). Fortunately, the SSI is currently in place and working well, because the AZ was discontinued after budget cuts in 2010. The AZ will be replaced by Project L.I.F.T. (Leadership and Investment For Transformation), a privately funded plan that represents over $55 million. Project L.I.F.T. is targeted to the West Charlotte corridor, which contains West Charlotte High School and its feeder middle and elementary schools. West Charlotte was selected due to its low graduation rate of 50 percent, which is significantly lower than the average CMS graduation rate of 70 percent.

Strategic Staffing Initiative

Peter Gorman was always interested in finding a way to better manage talent within his district. Shortly after he arrived, he asked the board what they thought about moving leaders and teachers involuntarily to the neediest schools. Prompted by the board's advice to rethink the strategy, he decided he would be more successful employing a "pull" strategy. He then had to consider the next logical question: "How do you get teachers who are perfectly happy where they are to voluntarily take a position in a chronically struggling school where student performance is low and there is a history of discipline problems and violence?" Gorman attacked that problem by convincing the board to approve cash incentives of $10,000 to $15,000 to teach in the four high schools cited previously by Howard Manning as part of the district's "academic genocide." However, that approach was not well structured and the poorly defined incentives were not used. Not to be deterred, Gorman was still convinced that the right "pull" strategy could be created, so he assembled leaders from accountability, human resources, and curriculum, as well as his chief academic officer, to develop the Strategic Staffing Initiative (SSI).

The initiative outlined a method for identifying the lowest-performing schools and the highest-performing principals, and then giving the high-performing principals incentives to lead those low-performing schools. The selected schools had chronic low student achievement, had qualified for restructuring, or had a poor-performing principal. To attract strong principals to those schools, Gorman announced the initiative (with great fanfare, according to an article in *Newsweek*) as a "competition" to identify the best principals.[4] Principals demonstrating the ability to achieve academic growth with students were selected for the "opportunity" to turnaround one of the district's failing schools. The principals would make a three-year commitment to that school, and in return would receive a 10 percent raise, freedom from some of the district's rules, and the ability to choose an eight-person transformation team, who would also receive raises. The seven principals selected for the first seven SSI schools accepted the positions. The expectations set for the principals were to raise student achievement by over a year's growth in one year's time, and to transform the culture of the school to expect high academic achievement. The district selected another seven principals for the second set of seven SSI schools.

The teams that principals were allowed to bring to their schools had a set structure. The positions they could fill included an assistant principal, a literacy facilitator, a behavior management technician, and up to five teachers with proven success. In addition to bringing in a team, principals were allowed to "prune existing staff," and could remove as many as five teachers, who were then reassigned.[5] To be selected by a principal for a SSI school, teachers had to have successful past summative evaluations and have shown growth in student achievement in reading and in math. If selected, teachers would receive a $10,000 recruitment bonus for a three-year commitment, plus a $5,000 retention bonus in the second and third years. In addition to the prestige of being selected by a principal to be an SSI teacher, one of the biggest draws for teachers was being able to work with a "validated" strong and effective principal.

When district leaders were ready to announce the initiative, they knew they had to carefully construct the messaging. Not only were the seven selected schools affected, but also seven other schools would be losing some of the district's strongest principals and teachers. Thus, Gorman and district leaders announced the initiative as being "important for improving the learning environment in some of our lowest-performing schools." Within that message, Gorman emphasized to the public the importance of having a districtwide commitment to *all* CMS schools. The first seven principals also backed the messaging, with one being quoted in a media briefing as saying,

"It's the moral thing to do. This is the single most ethical educational initiative I've ever been involved in as an educator."[6]

When results came in June 2009, the first cohort of principals had been in place for a year, and the second cohort for less than four months (timing and more details of the cohort placements are discussed later in the chapter). The state tests showed substantial growth at thirteen of the fourteen schools, ranging from 5- to 23-point increases in proficiency.

One way to ensure that SSI schools received what they needed from central office was to make certain the program was driven from a level where decisions could easily be made and resources leveraged. It is for that reason that the program is overseen by the chief academic officer (CAO) rather than HR. Having oversight by the CAO is important because the work spans curriculum, instruction, human resources, and many other supports for schools, making SSI a reform strategy rather than an HR strategy. Given that the CAO has more convening power over these departments than HR, it's a natural and logical fit. The CAO explained to central office staff that SSI schools come first. In her words, "They are considered 911 schools. They get the science kits first, curriculum assistance, whatever they need."

To date, SSI has completed three cohorts in 14 elementary schools, 5 middle schools, and 1 high school. Of the 20 schools, 19 are Title I, and all were deemed low-performing.

Figure 3.1 compares 2008–09 and 2009–10 composite reading and math scores in SSI scores. While the scores are relatively lower than the state and district average, they do show growth at all schools except one.

Figure 3.2 illustrates increases in composite reading and math scores for economically disadvantaged students from 2008–09 and 2009–10 at all SSI schools.

FIGURE 3.1

CMS Performance composite for previous two school years (reading and math)

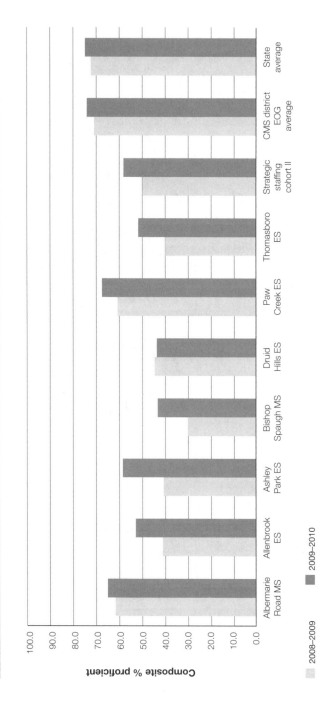

Composite % proficient

■ 2008–2009   ■ 2009–2010

Note: ES = elementary school; MS = middle school; HS = high school.

Source: Used with permission from Charlotte-Mecklenburg Schools.

FIGURE 3.2

CMS Economically disadvantaged proficiency for previous two school years (reading and math)

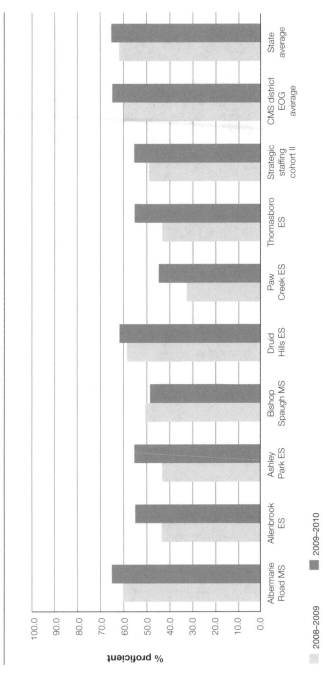

Note: ES = elementary school; MS = middle school; HS = high school.

Source: Used with permission from Charlotte-Mecklenburg Schools.

SUCCESSION PLANNING

While the SSI strategy appeared to be doing a good job of placing strong teachers and principals in high-need schools, CMS leaders also were well aware that shifting strong leaders and teachers out of schools left vacancies that needed to be filled with equal talent. Illustrating the potential scope of the problem, one district leader stated, "Can you imagine with twenty-five SSI schools, that's twenty-five opportunities for teachers and parents to get upset when we take their talent." To ensure the district had a viable pipeline of effective leaders and teachers from which to draw on, it developed a deliberate and systemic effort to better identify, train, and manage its talent.

When district leaders speak about succession planning, they are almost always referring to the development of a strong principal pipeline. However, in CMS, succession planning encompasses the entire system, including central office leaders—a smart but atypical practice. Gorman presented a succession plan to the board in 2010, explaining that it was critical to ensure the district had great principals and great district leaders for each department. Gorman wanted to be more intentional than "waiting for the right people to show up." He stressed the importance of identifying potential talented leaders and teachers, understanding their strengths and weaknesses, and developing them.[7] In CMS, succession planning meant that the district was committed to:

- Ensure continuity in key leadership positions
- Retain and develop intellectual capital for the future
- Encourage individual advancement

The three organizational levels addressed in the CMS talent pipeline include central office leaders, school leaders, and teachers.

The process for developing a pipeline in those three areas follows a uniform and cyclical structure:

- *Recruitment*: Processes to attract strong talent to avoid having to coach out teachers for poor performance later.
- *Data management systems*: Metrics and program evaluation to provide better and more real-time information to teachers, principals, and district leaders regarding performance.
- *Talent identification*: Succession planning to build talent pools, forced ranking leadership exercise, talent development discussions, and developing leadership competencies.
- *Leadership development*: Executive leadership development program and individualized leadership growth plans.
- *Performance management*: Midyear and end-of-year evaluations and measurable goals.

The overall succession management strategy is led by an employee who came to the district with an impressive business background, which included developing HR strategies and training for *Fortune* 500 companies.

One of the most interesting practices in the succession planning process is the identification of talent, which involves having district and school leaders go through a forced ranking and leadership exercise with their staff. The leader of this work told me that the process was borrowed from the business world and is used by Target, among other companies. When the forced ranking exercise was first introduced, eighty leaders in key positions were asked to force-rank their employees in one of four quartiles (which were also divided into quartiles for a total of

66

sixteen ranks) and rank from "4D" (which means having diffi-culty) to "1A" (which means the best among peers and immedi-ately promotable). The three dimensions that drove the rank-ing were planning, customer focus (with staff, students, and parents as the customer), and directing others. Within each category were subcategories, such as driving for results, written communication, political savvy, hiring and staffing, listening, peer relationships, and confronting direct reports. The ranking process included a strategy to replenish personnel who moved up the ranks; leaders were asked to train a specified percentage within a rank per promoted candidate.

Once candidates were ranked, they were sorted into a num-ber of programs. Top district leaders went into an executive leadership development program, called Leaders for Tomor-row, where they work on specific skills informed by an individ-ualized leadership growth plan. The program is associated with the principal pipeline, but it is also available for school leaders interested in becoming district leaders. There are also Effective School Leaders programs, which include training from Edu-cation Resource Strategies (ERS) for SSI leaders, the Principal Leadership Development, and principal preparation by either Leaders for Tomorrow or New Leaders for New Schools. Teach-ers also have leadership training opportunities in the Aspiring Leaders Program.

After principals practiced with the forced ranking instru-ment, they applied it to their teachers to see where each one would rank. This was an "eye-opening" exercise, according to one district leader, because he had the opportunity to view each teacher's ranking against his or her student achieve-ment growth scores and teacher evaluation. Overall, the pro-cess helped identify staff training needs and provided a much more nuanced system for reducing force as needed. Rather than depending on "last hired, first fired," the principals were given a tool to help them either develop or shed their lowest-performing teachers. The tool also motivated personnel to continue to grow and develop, because they knew that at any time they could fall down on ranking, even if they started at the top.

The interesting thing about the forced ranking process was how it was employed in central office. For example, if a curriculum director has ten employees, the director force-ranks those employees to identify who could eventually take over that position. Each employee is developed in his or her areas of weakness and then ranked again. Then, if the curriculum director were to leave, he or she could name a successor, and that person would be ready to assume the role. The tool was also used in finance, operations, and every major department at central office.

Before this process started, the district did not have a leader for the HR department; the work was being covered by the CAO and the succession planning director. However, when the district budget shifted at the beginning of the 2011–12 year, the district had to hire over five hundred teachers. Rather than rehire the teachers who had been "shed" because they were low performers, the district engaged the help of The New Teacher Project (TNTP) to help fill the positions and train district leaders on attracting and hiring the best candidates at the same time.[8] The beauty of this solution was that TNTP works at the national level and has data about where talented teachers have just lost positions through district downsizing. At the time I conducted the interviews, TNTP had already helped the district hire hundreds of teachers for CMS—proof that the district has a strong ability to engage effective partners.

Getting the right talent matched to unique positions is a difficult but very important task. The CAO spoke of the difficulty of filling a vacancy for a chemistry teacher and trying to balance "desperation with quality control." Rather than investing all its time managing that balance, CMS is working on having more systematic control over its talent pool. The CAO believes the succession planning has gone well, and that in about a year, the district will be able to say it has the right principal in every school—the result of its hard work in training people and focusing on "speaking the truth" when it comes to developing and supporting personnel. She also reported that she has seen much enthusiasm in the district around human capital exemplifying that excitement in her own description: "This is the exciting part about the potential role in a large urban district: to intentionally match people to positions. It resonates with how we think about our work."

CMS is working on refining its human capital strategy by striving to develop more comprehensive means to evaluate and compensate teachers. The district has been engaged with the Bill and Melinda Gates Foundation on the Measuring Effective Teachers (MET) project for three years. The project serves as an intensive research study to determine important questions about evaluating teachers, such as which is the best evaluation rubric to use, how many raters it takes to create reliable ratings, how do student survey results connect to teacher value-added scores, and what is the best way to observe and provide feedback to teachers. One of the cornerstones of the MET project that has been cited as being very effective in changing instruction is its process of videoing teacher lessons. During the project, MET teachers are asked to video four specific types of lessons, which are then sent to researchers who code the instruction (as part of the rater validity portion). The teacher gets to view the videos and is asked to write a reflection on what he or she saw. District leaders and teachers felt this was the most effective part of the MET project, and that it had really helped change instruction. An eight-year veteran teacher said: "I learned more on how I teach. My real focus is to slow down when I teach low-level readers. After watching myself, I was better able to break down the material for them and it was a lightbulb year—I made connections with them and had high growth scores. MET forced me to be more deliberate [in] how I taught things, more deliberate [in] how I approached material I had watched myself."

This teacher also mentioned that she realized she was calling on more girls than boys, and started to work on remediating that process. Though that portion of the study is over, CMS has been given another Gates grant to continue to use the videoing process. In addition to using the videos to help teachers reflect on their instruction, the district also plans to use them to share well-executed lessons for professional development.

CMS district leaders are now focusing on improving their teacher evaluation system and are waiting for the results from the MET study to inform the process. They have been developing a process to tie compensation to student growth for teachers, but are approaching the process carefully to ensure they are able to build the right payment and support structures, as well as a valid evaluation system that is embraced by principals and teachers.

PERFORMANCE MANAGEMENT

CMS has been working on developing its accountability framework to better understand performance across the district in tandem with their turnaround work. One refrain often heard in interviews at CMS is that Peter Gorman likes data, and when you speak to him, you "better know your data." To better understand school performance, the CMS office of accountability developed three tools to provide quantitative and qualitative data to identify successes and challenges in each school: School Progress Reports, School Quality Reviews, and School Improvement Plans.

School Progress Reports, developed in partnership with the RAND Corporation in March 2007, provide quantitative measures on student achievement and persistence. The reports include test scores, parent and student survey results, safety-audit results, and a letter from the principal. The end result is an assessment on progress each school is making toward its goals. To capture what principals described as "the nuances" in their buildings, the accountability office also developed School Quality Reviews (SQR) that captured more qualitative measures. The SQR entails a self-assessment based on a rubric that evaluates teaching and learning, curriculum, leadership and management, the learning environment, and parent/community involvement. The school is then visited by a Cambridge Education reviewer who interviews staff, teachers, parents, and students and conducts classroom observations. After the visit, the external review team creates a report identifying the school's strengths and weaknesses. Final reports are sent to the principal and area superintendent. Within thirty days, the principals share the results with the school and community, who identify the top two or three priorities to focus on from the report. The School Progress Reports and SQRs are used to develop School Improvement Plans, which are aligned to the district's overall strategic plan. The three-year School Improvement Plans are used to regularly monitor what is happening in schools and identify supports. The district brochure on CMS performance management states that these three tools are also helpful because they are key components of the principal evaluation and are continuously monitored by area superintendents.

Freedom and Flexibility with Accountability (FFA)

When Peter Gorman came to CMS, the district had shifted between decentralization and centralization a few times. To keep the right balance between oversight and innovation, Gorman and the board settled on their overarching approach of "freedom and flexibility with accountability." In application this meant that curriculum and instruction would be managed from central office, but with a balance between accountability and empowerment. A second part of this approach was the acknowledgment that all schools are not the same, and require different resources. Thus, central office pushed decision making back down to principals and held them accountable for results. Gorman surmised that the approach would help offset complaints heard from schools like "managed curriculum has sucked the soul out of teaching and learning." Gorman felt FFA gave him the opportunity to provide flexibility for someone who says, "I'd rather do it another way." FFA was first implemented in the 2008–09 school year with principals in twelve high schools, ten middle schools, and twenty-six elementary schools. They were encouraged to try practices that would work at their schools that might not work at other schools. Central office leaders encouraged principals to look at research, talk to experienced practitioners, and try innovative approaches, as long as they used the curriculum based on the state standards and got acceptable results.

For example, principals could choose to create gender-specific classes, double-block courses, or multi-age grouping. They could opt out of a planned district training for staff if they felt the school needed a school-based training to meet their own unique needs. Principals have three years to exercise the freedom, while district officials periodically review the school's progress to assess whether to endorse continued flexibility at that school. The district's long-range goal is to provide FFA to every principal, but central office leaders want to examine the results from the first pilot of schools first.

Data use and performance management have been a large part of CMS practices for the last ten years. As mentioned earlier, Peter Gorman was very interested in seeing data to understand every aspect that affected teaching and learning in the district. Achievement Zone and FOCUS schools receive training in Data Wise, an online student data system that is intended to sharpen educators' skills in analyzing and using student data to improve instruction and performance.[9] School Data Teams, facilitators, technology support, assistant principals for instruction, AZ teams, and Data Wise teams work with educators in the schools on the effective use of data to improve instruction. The Data Wise practices are integrated within the School Improvement Process and School Quality Review initiative. District leaders reported that Data Wise had been a key innovation for helping school staff deepen their understanding of how to use available data to improve instruction and student outcomes. In addition to those systems, CMS recently launched a districtwide formative, summative, and benchmarking system in 2010–11. The district signed a three-year contract with a vendor (Thinkgate) for the Web-based system, which offers online access to school and centrally based users.

PARTNERSHIPS

CMS did not use an external turnaround specialist to manage its improvement process. Rather, it has engaged various organizations, as it had in the past, to provide specific types of expertise like data training, leadership development, and teacher training. It has also engaged philanthropic organizations to assist with portions of the work. The partners CMS selects are well established in a specific area of expertise, and the district uses them to support strategies outlined in the strategic plan. To recruit teachers for high-need schools, CMS partners with Teach for America and the Charlotte Teachers Institute (in partnership with David College and UNC Charlotte). To open pathways for alternative leader and teacher routes, they partner with New Leaders for New Schools and The New Teacher Project. The Aspiring Leaders Program, Leaders for Tomorrow (with Winthrop University), Queens University Leadership Institute, and Education Resource Strategies are some of the main partners used to develop leadership talent in the district. The Parthenon Group has worked with the district on developing and implementing its 2014 strategic plan. Additionally, the district is beginning to investigate partnerships with historically African American colleges and universities to add diversity to its educator corps.

CLIMATE AND CULTURE

Interviews with CMS personnel at all system levels reveal a culture that values accountability and transparency and is focused on improvement. Having seen the needle move in schools where it has been stuck for years has encouraged the adults in the system to continue to dig in, keep focused and aligned, and work together toward student improvement. One district leader said, "This district is comfortable with discomfort. If there is an issue, we will put it out there and vet it to death. There is transparency here, and we are kept accountable, which I think is healthy." Transparency was also mentioned as being important for leading to what many referred to as "crucial conversations."

CHALLENGES AND CHANGES

Several ongoing and future challenges came up in district interviews. One challenge was that some members of the district community questioned whether the district was providing equity for students and schools. District leaders felt that not everyone understood the difference between *equity* and *equality*, and that providing every student and school with equal resources would not result in equitable education opportunities. Several leaders mentioned that there were some community members, both internal and external, who felt cheated when they did not receive the immediate attention or resources that the AZ, FOCUS, or SSI schools received. A second, larger challenge was the impending end of funds that covered the stipend for teachers in the SSI schools, as it was only budgeted for three years. District leaders were working on how to resolve that issue and help SSI principals retain their teachers.

Another big challenge was that in the summer of 2011, Peter Gorman announced that he was leaving the district to work in the private sector. When asked how his leaving will affect the district, he responded that it would not, as the district's turnaround and overall strategic plan was built on a strong foundation with the right personnel in place to execute the plan. In an interview, Gorman said he has been working with the CMS board to ensure that the candidate they ultimately select is the right fit to carry out the successful plans already in motion.

VIEW FROM SCHOOLS

Being selected as a principal for an SSI school is seen as an honor in CMS. The CAO in Charlotte noted that principals were openly disappointed when they were not selected for an SSI school. Two SSI principals talked with me about their experience in the first cohort of SSI. Both had come from affluent suburban schools, which surprised me at first, until one explained, "It's easier to gain experience in an excellent school than in a struggling school." They were honored and excited to be selected, and one confessed that as soon as she became a principal, she had already had "the itch to move" because she wanted to work in turnaround schools.

In their first year, the Cohort I principals went into their schools in July, which they felt (and the district acknowledges) was problematic, because they did not get a chance to see each school "in action." One principal said the cohort structure was helpful because the initiative was new, and she found it to be useful for providing support and ideas. Another described the process of going into her SSI school at first as, "Difficult. You don't know who to trust and they don't want you there, and it feels uncomfortable." At another school, the principal found a culture that was "nice enough," but had no sense of urgency.

To address the timing issue and provide SSI principals with more time to observe when the school was in the session,

Cohort II started in their new schools on March 1, 2009. When the Cohort II principals started, the former principals left the schools and were either dismissed or demoted. The other selected members of the team would join the school at the beginning of the next academic year.

After Cohort II had been underway for a while, the district made some other adjustments. One was to eliminate the behavior management technician position. Another was to make the stipulation that only teachers on improvement plans could be reassigned elsewhere by an SSI principal.

For Cohort III, which started in 2010–11, the district hired Education Resource Strategies (ERS) to create a more structured process to prepare principals to enter SSI schools. ERS focused this training with the principals on context, vision, and design.[10]

The principals interviewed agreed that the new timeline begun with Cohort II was better and allowed them to observe for a few months, set goals, determine professional development for staff, and then hire over the summer. One said she was able to have a staff retreat in July to prepare for the next year, discuss what the "new" school would look like, and do team building.

When asked what they did first in their new schools, one SSI principal talked about the importance of going in with a goal and a plan and not getting distracted by anything else. She changed the whole master schedule and worked with teachers on instruction, and "people knew it was serious." This principal felt it was important to signal early in turnaround schools that things would change. She made sure that teachers understood what and how to teach and what the goals were for the school. The building was cleaned up, and students were brought to visit the local college to further ramp up their expectations.

Teachers and students set goals and milestones, had benchmark assessments every four weeks, had behavioral goals, and got a new mascot to represent their new school and culture.

This principal's efforts at her new school paid off. When she began, her school had a composite score of 24 percent, with 12 percent proficiency in science, 18 percent in reading, and 24 percent in math. After the first year, the composite score was 44 percent, and the school made AYP and expected growth. The other principal's school started at 45 percent composite proficiency, with 35 percent in reading and 48 percent in math. By March of that year, the school had a composite score of 56 percent, and then 64 percent the next year. The school is now off the state's school improvement list and has made AYP.

CONCLUSION

District leaders in Charlotte-Mecklenburg all believe that schools can be turned around, and most of those I interviewed thought the SIG program was helpful in creating urgency and support for chronically failing schools. However, several interviewees did not believe that school turnaround could or should be boiled down into specific models.

CMS's more formalized turnaround strategy started with a strong foundation in a system that already valued human capital, high-quality instruction, accountability, continuous performance monitoring, and some amount of community support. Peter Gorman, who led the turnaround, believed that it was important to intervene early, and by putting struggling schools together to function as a professional learning community—the Achievement Zone—the district was able to better differentiate and manage focus and supports for those schools.

The approach the district took drilled down into the four required strategies outlined in the SIG's transformation model: teacher and leader effectiveness, comprehensive instructional reform strategies, extended learning time and community-oriented schools, and providing flexibility and support.

CMS also believed that turnaround should "raise the tide and all the ships" rather than focus only on the most struggling schools. To this end, it did a good job bringing together its targeted elements to create a coherent strategy that yielded positive improvement across the district, and particularly in those schools. As a result, the district won the Broad Prize for Urban Education in 2011.

While CMS did a great job focusing on flexibility within accountability and performance monitoring, the strongest implementation of its program was through their far-reaching human capital strategies, which were bold, innovative, and identified strong and weak district and school leaders and teachers. Through its forced ranking system, CMS helped better define expectations and effective performance, pointed out weaknesses and remedied them when possible, and removed staff who did not meet those expectations. While the district's strategic staffing strategy and succession planning are great models for others to examine and consider, it would be very important for other systems, particularly those that operate in conjunction with strong teacher unions, to consider if their systems can create the same flexibility to incentivize, rank, improve, and remove personnel using a similar approach.

4

SCHOOL DISTRICT OF PHILADELPHIA

*Noteworthy practice area: Parent involvement.
Recently resigned superintendent made a substantial
impact on a large segment of parents by teaching them how
to advocate for an "appropriate" education.*

Chapter Highlights
- Turnaround strategy targeted ninety-five schools using three different models that included charter management organizations.
- Major focus on students, raising accountability, human capital strategies, and community engagement.
- High level of political and financial struggles.

BACKGROUND

The eighth-largest school district in the nation, the School District of Philadelphia (Philadelphia), serves the entire city of Philadelphia and has an enrollment of almost 155,000 students. The demographics are diverse, with 58.3 percent of students being African American, 7 percent Asian, 13.8 percent White, 18 percent Hispanic, and 3 percent "other."[1] The district serves a number of schools, with 171 elementary, 25 middle, and 61 high schools. Additionally, through one of the reform structures detailed shortly, the district has 74 charter schools.

The district was governed by a mayor-appointed board until 2001, when it was taken over by the state. As a result, a new governing body, the School Reform Commission (SRC), was created. The takeover gave the governor the power to appoint three of the five members of the SRC; the remaining two members were to be appointed by the mayor. Understanding the district's past and current conflicts is important, as politics still seem to have a stronghold on its ability to set the course for school reform. Some of the district's most challenging struggles fall under finance, governance, charters, and relationships.

Philadelphia school finance has suffered the same equity issues as other districts where funding relies on property taxes. Conflict over spending inequities had been an issue since 1975, but things erupted in 2000 when it came to light that the surrounding suburban districts had much higher per-pupil funding; with numbers like $12,076 and $13,288 per student, compared with Philadelphia's $6,969.[2] Additionally, because property values were too low for the district to compensate for loss of state funds, David Hornbeck, the superintendent in 2000, threatened to close down schools and adopt an unbalanced budget if the city would not help make up the funding gap. Turmoil over two court cases ensued, and the situation was resolved by then mayor John F. Street, who negotiated a "friendly" state takeover of the district.[3] In June 2000,

Hornbeck ended his six-year service in Philadelphia, stating that he did not think he had the financial support to improve the district's schools.

Feeling that it did not have the resources or capacity to improve its large number of failing schools, the district launched a diverse service provider approach by using several outside organizations. The provider model included proposals to partner with charter management organizations (CMOs) as well as district management operators like Edison Schools. Prompted by concern over ownership and control, a segment of the community teamed up with labor unions to form the Coalition to Keep Our Public Schools Public. One major action taken by that group was to file a lawsuit against Edison Schools, which was being considered to help manage central office and a number of schools. When Paul Vallas became superintendent, he reversed the decision to engage Edison because he saw managing central office as his role. Other external providers that were contracted to work with the district included Universal Companies, Victory Schools, Foundations Inc., and the University of Pennsylvania. In 2005, Vallas implemented a plan to turn over a number of schools to Mastery Charter Schools.

It is against this backdrop of multiple providers, concerns about financial equity, numerous schools not making AYP, union leaders trying to keep their members out of charters and within the folds of the district, and a politically appointed governing body that Arlene Ackerman became Philadelphia's district leader in 2008. Despite her abruptly shortened tenure (after three years, Ackerman's recently approved four-year contract was bought out by the district in September 2011) and the unearthing of political backroom charter contract deals resulting in the resignation of two SRC members, the district has fared pretty well. Data for 2010 show:

- 158 schools (59 percent of the district) made AYP, 33 percent more than the previous year (119 in 2009).
- 34 percent of Empowerment schools made AYP, up from 22 percent in 2009.
- More than half the city's students meet state standards (50.7 percent reading; 56.6 percent math) for the first time.
- Violent incidents dropped by 29 percent.[4]

TURNAROUND STRATEGY

Philadelphia's turnaround strategy is built on its Strategic Plan 2014, which is designed to meet district goals of being student-centered, having strong accountability, and creating a close connection between the community and schools. Arlene Ackerman's view of turnaround came from her understanding that the district's issues were not isolated around the more than ninety struggling schools. Rather, the district had a high illiteracy rate, and parents were not particularly happy with their neighborhood schools. According to Ackerman, "Seventy-six percent of kids select a high school outside of their neighborhood because they don't think they have good schools where they live." Thus, the district's turnaround model was "not as much about changing one local school as it was about changing geographical pathways and changing entire communities." Ackerman also stated that she was not as interested in closing down schools as she was in improving all the schools in the system. She described that process as "a systemic approach from bottom up and top down. The district's role is to remove barriers to systemic change in learning that is inclusive of parents and community so that the end is real investment in the schools' success." The main divisions of the plan and parts that I believe support and enhance its turnaround strategy are:

1. *Student success*: The focus is on yearly student growth and skills for success in college, work, and life through:
   - Clear and uniform teaching standards and expectations for teachers
   - Professional development on differentiated instruction, academic rigor, and using data to inform instruction
   - Teachers working in collaborative teams
   - Coaches for teachers
   - Early warning indicator system to support struggling students
   - Regional Newcomer Center to support new immigrant students
   - Stronger parent and family engagement through communication, Parent Resource Centers, and Parent University
   - School-level (preschool, elementary, middle, and high school) specific strategies (too numerous to be detailed in the scope if this book, but worth examining)

2. *Quality choices*: Building a system of schools where success is rewarded and parents have a variety of options:
   - Performance management system with uniform standards and evaluations for the entire district, charters, and contract schools
   - Rewarding high-performing schools with greater autonomy and replicating their success (Vanguard schools)

- Restructuring and transforming consistently low-performing schools (Renaissance schools)
- Providing quality choices to students and parents and ensuring a transparent and inclusive decision-making process that engages students, parents, and the community

3. *Great staff*: To have talented staff that reflects the diversity of the student body:
   - Recruit the best candidates in a timely way
   - Open an Office of Teacher Affairs to support and advocate for teachers
   - Create Professional Development Centers
   - Create leadership institutes for aspiring leaders
   - Implement a new standards-based evaluation process for teachers, principals, district staff, and managers

4. *Accountable adults*: To ensure employees understand what they are accountable for:
   - Implement performance measures for all schools and departments tied to evaluations to meet system-wide goals
   - Publish annual progress reports for all schools and the district
   - Design strategic compensation packages to reward high performance
   - Identify and require common standards of professionalism

5. *World-class operations*: To provide best business and operational practices and support equality and the district's mission:
  - "Right-size" facilities and provide fair resource allocation
  - Align budget with district goals
  - Develop a weighted student funding formula

Outlining how this plan drives turnaround is important, as it illustrates comprehensive alignment with overall district goals and strategies rather than add-on programs driven at the school level. Ackerman began her first year in the district in September 2008 by announcing her plan to address eighty-five underperforming schools (in 2011, the number was raised to ninety-five). Over the past three years, the plan has been revised to create a tiered intervention approach and add more delivery options to meet school and student needs, make midcourse corrections, and address the challenges mentioned above.

In 2008, the first low-performance intervention tier was referred to as Empowerment schools, to connote the district's commitment to "empower" schools by directly providing resources and supports to them. A school became an Empowerment school if it had not met AYP under NCLB guidelines and was in Corrective Action Level II.[5] Additionally, schools received a ranking based on two numbers: where they were (1) compared with the district and (2) compared with similar schools. A school ranked 1/1 was a top-performing school in the district; 10/10 was at the bottom. Hoping that the additional focus would spark more aggressive improvement, the district designated the Empowerment schools to receive individualized professional development, scripted programs to build basic academic skills, quarterly assessments in reading and math, a parent ombudsman, a student adviser, additional volunteers, and the assistance of the Empowerment School Response (ESR) teams. Additionally, twenty-three of the most struggling school within the eighty-five would also receive a social service liaison, an instructional specialist, a full-time substitute teacher, a part-time retired principal, increased nursing services, and additional monthly walk-throughs.[6]

The fifteen ESR teams of trained educators, working with staff in ten regions and at central headquarters, were a main component of the Empowerment model. They continually monitored for alignment and progress through frequent meetings with regional superintendents. Results on the Empowerment schools thus far look positive; in the 2009–10 school year, 34 percent of the Empowerment schools made AYP, many of them for the first time in a very long history of failure.

In 2010, the district announced a more intensive intervention for schools that were still not moving the needle despite the extra resources and supports. Empowerment schools that do not improve become Renaissance Alert schools (marking the shift to the new model), signaling that the next year the school may be eligible for one of several Renaissance school models. If there is still no improvement, the school will take one of two paths: become a Promise Academy, or a Renaissance Match school, where it will work with an external CMO. According to Ackerman, during the first year of implementation, schools applied for the model they preferred. During the second year, the decision was driven more by the district, because it was attempting to create more turnaround feeder patterns.

There is some difference in terminology used for Renaissance schools; the district refers to the turnaround schools still under its control as Promise Academies, and the other models managed externally as Renaissance schools. However, in some documents and on the district FAQ sheets, all schools are under the *Renaissance* label, with the Promise Academy name embedded under that. The big difference between the two models is that Promise Academies are under district control, and Renaissance schools are not. Renaissance schools are run by CMOs, which hire their own staff and teachers. Thirteen schools were served in the first year of the Renaissance strategy. In the second year, the diversity of models was opened up and is described next.

Promise Academies

Traditional Promise Academies provide additional learning time and are built on private school concepts. They offer longer school days Monday through Thursday, Saturday classes, and summer academies. Extra resources, like field trips, uniforms, and a staff dress code, are provided to promote a positive image. Addressing needs of students and their families is a major component and is accomplished by the presence of a full-time parent ombudsman, student adviser, social service liaison, full-time nurse, and a resource specialist. The culture focuses on university attendance through college and career exploration with local colleges. When a school transitions to the traditional Promise model, up to 51 percent of original school staff members may remain and the principal may remain if he or she was at school fewer than two years. Six schools were managed by the district under the traditional Promise model in the 2010–11 school year.

The Promise Academy innovation model was designed for underperforming schools that had already introduced reforms and were showing positive growth under new leadership. The Promise Innovation model had many of the same features as the traditional model, with the addition of a weeklong summer institute and an hour a day for professional and academic development. Several schools that applied to follow the Innovation model were denied because they lacked an established academic track record. The next year, no schools applied, and the district decided to discontinue it, since it was very similar to the traditional Promise model. However, according to one local newspaper, terminating that model elicited some pushback, since it provided more instructional oversight and flexibility than the traditional model, which employed highly scripted remedial programs like SRA Corrective Reading.

Because she found high schools to be difficult to change, Arlene Ackerman created a pathway to address school feeder patterns, which became Promise Neighborhood Schools, modeled after the Harlem Children's Zone. Funded by a federal grant, the Promise Neighborhood Schools are managed by the district in partnership with Universal Companies and are designed to provide cradle-to-career services to families in the South Philadelphia neighborhood. The approach aspires to move into the neighborhood and have schools become a part of the culture and solution for community improvement. For example, Universal bought a dilapidated building to construct an outside playground for children. The goal is to "try to fix dysfunctional communities" and reach out to parents and families. Universal, founded by music recorder Kenny Gamble, wanted to do something to "get the African American community off its knees." In January 2011, Ackerman announced that if the first Promise

Neighborhood School went well, more neighborhoods would be targeted for a similar approach.

Data on Promise Academies show that between the 2009–10 and 2010–11 school years, most schools reduced out-of-school suspensions and had significant reductions in violent incidents. The schools also showed an increase in academic achievement. Figure 4.1 shows that all six schools increased in benchmark reading proficiency exams between Spring 2010 and Fall 2010.

Renaissance Schools

Instead of closing down schools and farming out students, schools earmarked for the Renaissance Match model kept their students and brought in a CMO that selected and hired its own staff, who became employees of the organization rather than

FIGURE 4.1

Comparison of Spring 2010 and Fall 2010 Promise Academies reading

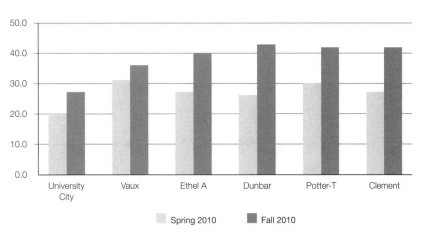

Source: Used with permission from The School District of Philadelphia.

the district (although they have been allowed to pause their union membership rather than lose it entirely). To manage a Renaissance Match school, the CMO participates in a competitive bid process managed by each school's School Advisory Council (SAC). To select the CMO, the SAC, composed of 51 percent parents and then teachers, principals, and a community person, oversee the request for qualifications process. They hear presentations from the charter organizations, visit schools to see them in action, host a question-and-answer session, and then vote for their top three choices. The superintendent and SRC make the final selection from those choices. Once a CMO is selected, it is approved for five years by the SRC. After five years, the SRC reviews the progress and decides whether to renew the contract. In every case but two (one part of the recent controversy described later in this chapter), the school's top CMO choice has been selected.

In 2010, the first year of the initiative, there were seven Renaissance schools—six elementary and one middle school. Universal Companies ran two of the schools, Mastery Charter Schools ran three, Young Scholars Charter School ran one, and ASPIRA ran the middle school. During the current (2011–12) school year, there are five Year II Renaissance schools, with Mosaica Education running an elementary, Mastery running an elementary and a high school, and ASPIRA running two high schools.

The charters are seen somewhat as competition to the district; they receive funds for Average Daily Attendance (ADA), and the teachers are no longer members of the union. One district leader noted that the state used to make up for some of the lost ADA funds; however, this year it reduced that funding. Ackerman stated in several interviews that she did not care who improved the schools, as long as they improved.

The chief executive officer of Universal Companies, Rahim Islam, described many characteristics of his school that mirror common well-proven strategies: "tons" of interventions for students based on data, personalized education, and different programs like arts and music to engage students. One of the main differences cited by Islam was Universal's management approach, which is grounded more in business than traditional education. In Universal schools, the principal is considered the "chief manager" of a school and works with a team that also includes a chief instructor. The schools' roles are essentially split between instruction and noninstruction. Assistant principals deal with noninstructional roles such as climate, safety, food service, and maintenance. The principal and instructional leaders are in charge of everything related to academics. Both instructional and noninstructional sides of the house work together to ensure they are moving "lock stock together" around academic goals, and student progress is constantly monitored. Schools run by Universal aspire to be a primary resource to the community, which Islam describes as "bringing the community into the school, and taking the school out to the community." There is a family resource center manager and case managers who closely monitor discipline and attendance and conduct home visits when necessary. The family resource center is open for extended hours and provides adult education, skills training, job preparation, and case management to students and their families.

When asked what kind of changes Islam sees when Universal takes over a school, he said, "I see dramatic change—within two weeks—in everything." He described a recent visit he made to one of his large schools (seven hundred students). When he went in, everything was quiet, and he wondered if there was a holiday he hadn't known about, because he did not see any students in the hallways or hear loud noises. But when he looked around, he saw all the students in the classrooms, wearing their school uniforms. He said that in the past they would have been running around in the hallways and fighting; now they were in classrooms learning. Islam also sees school pride. He explained, "I knew they were proud of their schools, because they wore their uniforms five or seven blocks away from school. I saw them walking home three and four kids deep across the sidewalk, looking respectful. They didn't take those jackets or ties off. They were proud of what they had on." Islam offered that the verdict is still out on community impact, but he is hopeful that in time those changes will come as well.

Stetson Middle School, a Phase I Renaissance school that used to be on the state's persistently dangerous list, is another school that was dramatically changed by its CMO, ASPIRA, Inc. ASPIRA began by cleaning up the building, giving it a fresh coat of paint and better lighting, and bringing in teachers two weeks early to make sure they were on the same page. ASPIRA engaged parents in the building remodel plan and the painting and spent time explaining its approach and expectations for students. The district charter division leader said that it was important that the school get the culture right to be successful "right out of the gate."

The main difference found between Promise Academies and Renaissance schools was that the charter-led Renaissance schools had more autonomy around how they managed human capital. As one district leader said, they had "less red tape" to cut through when hiring, could bring teachers in early if needed, and could be flexible with scheduling and instruction. Meanwhile, in the summer of 2011, teachers in Promise

Academies hung in limbo, waiting to find out if they would be protected from district layoffs. The Philadelphia Federation of Teachers (PFT) union applied for and got a temporary restraining order to stop teacher layoffs while the union and district battled in court. The district wanted the Promise teachers to be exempt from layoffs because of their commitment to the schools and specialized training. Additionally, most of the Promise Academy teachers were new, meaning that a "last hired, first fired" layoff strategy would decimate the staff in many Promise Academies. The union wanted the district to lay off newer teachers—if they had to lay off teachers at all. Many of the teachers could not wait until they received word, because other teacher jobs were being snapped up during the summer.

HUMAN CAPITAL

One of the important targets of the Strategic Plan 2014 is to have "great staff." Teacher development was not frequently referenced in interviews, perhaps because the focus of interviewees was the turnaround models themselves, or because mainly district and school leaders were interviewed, or because human capital strategies are somewhat limited in a strong union state like Pennsylvania. The district has implemented numerous practices to support teachers, all of which are likely helpful. These include ensuring schools have common planning time for teachers to meet, consolidating teacher services covering everything "from hiring to retirement" under the Office of Teacher Affairs, developing a plan to streamline hiring practices (an electronic applicant tracking system that was put on hold due to the budget crunch), planning to recruit teachers of color (also put on hold due to budget constraints), and implementing several grow-your-own teacher programs. Although the district felt pleased to have won some flexibility in the union contract for principals to be able to hire their own teachers, almost every leader interviewed mentioned that veteran teachers did not want to teach in Promise Academies, even with the incentives offered and the opportunity to earn more pay by working extended hours. Overall, the lack of veteran teachers in Promise Academies created some large staffing gaps for the schools that lost many new teachers to due to seniority-driven layoffs.

While the teacher pipeline practices were relatively traditional, district leaders understood that turning around chronically failing schools requires a completely different skill set and personality than maintaining them. One central office leader referred to successful turnaround principals as "Green Beret leaders." Accordingly, the district was working on identifying strong turnaround leaders and was moving principals with a successful turnaround track record to the most struggling schools. One principal interviewed was being moved to a new school after two years at his Promise Academy. Though he had not envisioned leaving his school, he seemed to understand he was needed and was up to the challenge. When asked if what he had put in place in his school would unravel, he said no, that he felt good about the principal who replaced him.

To improve the leader pipeline, the district had started a leadership development program, with forty hopeful leaders meeting monthly to learn from and train with the associate superintendent of schools. Training and maintaining the pipeline was a priority in the district, as well as focusing on matching people's skills to their positions.

CURRICULUM AND INSTRUCTION

Despite no mention of specific instructional approaches used in Philadelphia, most leaders did describe how instruction was addressed or improved. In one school, the principal spoke about focusing on cross-discipline, hands-on projects aimed at raising instructional rigor while connecting class work to the real world. Students in Promise Academies and Renaissance schools had extended school days, and Promise Academies offered enrichment classes on Saturdays; these included fencing and art, in addition to academics. Students were attracted to the classes, and attendance for them was very high, according to one principal.

Another principal related how he worked on creating a college-going culture in his K–8 school. He considered how the instructional program was implemented, and made sure his teachers were teaching lessons at the appropriate level. In his words, "I don't want to walk in and just see kindergarteners coloring. While they are coloring they can also work on numbers and writing letters."

PERFORMANCE MANAGEMENT

There was so much happening in the district during the time of the interviews that performance management was not explicitly probed; nor did the issue come up frequently, except that it was obvious that district and school leaders and teachers valued data and wanted to closely monitor progress. When principals described their strategies within their schools, most sentences started with, "We looked at the data and . . ." Additionally, there seemed to be a fair amount of transparency, as it is easy to find detailed interim and annual reports on the strategic plan and on district and school performance.

CLIMATE AND CULTURE

The climate of the district at the time of writing this chapter (late August–September 2011) was one of focus but wariness. Arlene Ackerman's contract had been bought out, layoffs were still being completed in central office, and many schools had experienced significant layoffs. When leaders were asked about the uncertainty of the district with no leader, responses were surprisingly void of concern or complaints. It seemed as though everyone was prepared to continue implementing the strategic plan. When I asked one principal how all the negative media attention, Ackerman's leaving, and the turmoil around losing so many Promise teachers was affecting the district, he responded, "In Philly, people are really strong mentally; they are not easily let down. They may be disappointed, but they'll bounce back really quickly. The children bounce back, and the toughest students became our top students."

While there was a lot of energy around and encouragement of the progress made in the Promise Academies and Renaissance schools—that performance was improving for the first time in years—there was also a lot of pushback about the schools for a number of reasons. Some stakeholders felt that Ackerman held the schools up as her "pet project." Others voiced resentment about the turnaround schools getting more than their fair share of attention and resources, a theme that recurs throughout the cases in this book. Characterizing the district's constant struggle between equity and equality, one district leader said, "That [finance equity] is the biggest public misconception around any school reform, why one gets more than the other. But they don't consider what the underlying root causes is. That's where the outcry is, they want to know, what will I lose at my school. People will say they want schools to improve, but at the end of the day they don't want to take away teachers or change anything that they think will risk their child's performance." He illustrated his point by using the metaphor of a doctor's office, where one would not expect everyone to get the same treatment: "If I had cancer and you had strep, we wouldn't expect to get the same attention or treatment."

RELATIONSHIPS AND PARTNERSHIPS— CHARTERS AND PARENTS

The main partnerships the district engages in are with the CMOs—Universal, Mosaic, Mastery, and ASPIRA. Interviews with district leaders and one charter CFO did not reveal a lot of interaction between charter and district staff; however, Arlene Ackerman said that recently the charter leaders and district leaders got together to discuss approaches to turning around low-performing schools. The new format of Renaissance feeder patterns was growing into more of an opportunity for charter/district interaction, and Universal's CEO, Rahim Islam, said he and the leaders of district-run schools in his neighborhood were meeting on a quarterly basis. One principal in a feeder pattern (jointly led by the district and a CMO) Renaissance school mentioned meeting monthly with the other principals in the chain of schools. They scheduled these meetings at each other's schools and set an agenda focused on a learning purpose that usually involved some observation in the school. Though there was not a lot of interaction at this point between the charters and district-led schools, one district leader asserted that the district felt it was learning from the CMOs. When asked what the charters did differently that might be useful, she stated that the charters did a particularly good job "marketing" their brand and mission, something she said the district had not really thought about. In her words, "They are very good at marketing their products; they talk about mastery. It becomes a brand for them; they sell it. We have to sell what we do well and communicate more with the community." Outside of the CMOs, Arlene Ackerman said the district did not engage with a specific turnaround partner because she saw herself as a turnaround specialist, thus eliminating the need for that type of external assistance. When asked what she thought of her charter partners, Ackerman said she resisted them at first, worried that they would cherry-pick their students. However, she found they worked well with the neighborhood children in their schools, and she felt it was "fair to have an open market" when it comes to reforming schools. Regardless of whether the approach was district- or charter-led, she said she just wanted good schools for parents and for parents to feel that their children were safe.

Although not traditionally classified in the same "partner" bucket, Ackerman often said, and seemed to truly believe, that parents were the district's main partners. While most districts do acknowledge the importance of parents, she truly saw them as one of the key levers if not *the* key lever in turning around schools. She cited two reasons for this belief: parents are necessary to create pressure from outside of the system for change, and parents select houses because of schools, so schools should have a positive connection to parents and their neighborhood.

Many programs put into place for parents in Philadelphia appeared to do a good job at providing needed services and drawing parents into the school, including:

- *Parent Resource Centers*: Eight centers located across the district to create easily accessible and timely resources for parents. Parents are guaranteed a response rate from the district within sixty hours of their request.
- *Parent University*: Provides opportunities for parents to strengthen parenting skills and knowledge. Included free of charge are parenting classes and workshops, family literacy and health and wellness courses, multilingual programs and certificates, professional certification, and college degree attainment. In 2010, the parent university had over nineteen thousand parents participating—six times as many as the previous year.
- *Superintendent's Parent Roundtable*: The superintendent meets with parents to discuss parent involvement and answer their concerns six times a year. The meetings have been moved to an auditorium because over eight hundred parents attend to hear Ackerman.
- *Parent school tours*: Before a Promise Academy opens, the parents at that school are taken on a bus by district leaders and shown a better-performing school in their neighborhood.

Parent involvement can be difficult, and it seemed to be one of Ackerman's strongest suits—partly, she said, because she was a single mother for many years, and thus felt like she could relate to some of their hardships. She said, "I knew what it was like to be too tired to look at your child's homework. So I'd tell the parents, 'If you are too tired one night, just write a note on it and have your signature there.' It's something." She wanted to meet parents "where they are" and inform them about advocating for their children.

One thing that frustrated Ackerman was that the money provided by Title I for parents with children in low-performing schools to switch to a better-performing school rolled over each year because parents didn't know it was an option. Therefore, in her roundtable meetings, she focused on providing information and skills to parents. She would tell them what to look for and demand from their school and how to demand it. She also told parents they needed to show up to get what they wanted, suggesting that they go to board meetings and observe in the classroom. If parents told her they were too busy, she suggested they team up with several other parents to take turns observing all of their children's classrooms.

Ackerman and other district leaders all understood that parents were operating from a framework of what they knew; that they were nervous but wanted a good education for their children. Both she and Francisco Duran, an area superintendent, took parents in buses to show them what a "good" school looks like, because "they probably did not go to one themselves and have never seen one." Duran said it was amazing to watch the parents look in awe at the schools. Ackerman and Duran would tell them, "See, this is what it should look like. This is what you should be pushing for. This is what you should see in your child's school."

Ackerman built great trust with Philadelphia's parents, and she would tell them in the roundtable meetings, "You can tell me anything, and it is my job to solve our problem in forty-eight hours." She described one meeting where parents told her they wanted to observe their children's classrooms but were told they could not come in without an appointment. She told the parents that was not a district rule and gave out her cell phone number, telling them, "You call me if that happens." The next morning, a parent called, and after Ackerman called the principal and explained that it was not a district policy, the principal invited the parent in to observe the class.

When news got out that Ackerman was leaving (the circumstances are described below), she said many parents cried. She said she told them, "The way you can honor me is to keep up the fight. It's not about me anymore. It's about what I stand for and you should stand for; if you fight for that change, then it can happen." She continued, "In a while, nobody will know who Arlene is, but the change that can happen will be there." Now that she has left the district, Ackerman says she plans to continue to focus on educating parents on advocating for their children. An article in the *Philadelphia Public School Notebook*, an electronic journal that covers education issues, published quotes from various leaders either praising or criticizing her. One quote by a community leader about Ackerman's relationships with parents and the community read: "Her main legacy was standing up for Black children so that they have the opportunity to get educated like all other children . . . Also, her willingness to take on the high schools as part of the reforms by turning University City and Vaux [schools] into Promise Academies. And her outreach to parents, her willingness to have conversations with parents. Those three things separate her from other superintendents."

Ask any central office or school leader in Philadelphia who the most important partner is to them, and more than likely they will say parents. Whether the district is able to stabilize during this period of leadership shifts and maintain its hard-won successes remains to be seen. However, even if every program is overturned, Dr. Ackerman's leadership will leave a legacy of newly empowered parents who had never been so closely connected to the schools.

CHANGES AND CHALLENGES

The three largest challenges in the district were politics, budget cuts, and personnel issues. A lot was going on in Philadelphia between August and September of 2011, and the newspapers ran headlines about political fallout almost daily. The superintendent who had led a number of chronically failing schools into a positive upswing was removed, SRC leaders resigned after a public unveiling of an attempted under-the-table charter operator contract, and the district suffered some deep budget cuts.

Some of the early falling out between the union and Arlene Ackerman occurred at the beginning of 2010, though at first she and other district leaders felt they had unprecedented support from the union for their turnaround approach. However, sometime in 2010, Ackerman said, the union leaders started voicing opposition to the Renaissance schools, perhaps because they felt they were losing membership to the charters. To appease the union, Ackerman flipped her plans and targeted more low-performing schools to be Promise Academies rather than Renaissance schools. She said she was shocked at the union's change of attitude, as they had also changed their opinion about Promise Academies, citing issues with merit and extra pay and lack of acknowledgement for seniority.

Whether attributed to pushback on the turnaround models or budget woes, the district also cut the number of new Promise Academies for the 2011–12 school year from eleven to three, for a total of nine. The Promise Academies also lost their extra instructional time on Saturdays, and the extra instructional hour during the week. One of the worst hits they took was the loss of the lawsuit that would have protected the many new teachers selected, trained, and successfully started at a Promise Academy. The lawsuit was ended in mid-August of 2011, and many new teachers at Promise Academies were laid off or had taken other jobs because they could wait no longer.

One Promise Academy teacher interviewed for the *Notebook* related how, because he couldn't afford to continue to wait after August to find out if he still had a job, he had to quit. However, he told the reporter that he was very upset and disappointed, because he had wanted to teach at the Academy and had enjoyed it, and now that same school has twenty job openings, which he cannot take because he's already on contract elsewhere.[7] Some principals mentioned that staff at Promise Academies with high concentrations of young teachers were "decimated." Other articles in the *Notebook* featured stories outlining school and community concern that the very teachers who needed to go would be back to fill all those vacant positions.

While concern was voiced about the cuts, several leaders felt strongly that money was not an excuse for the momentum to stop in Philadelphia. One principal said that even if he lost his entire budget, he would "still focus intensely on instruction, and still have students go to the bathroom on a schedule, single-file in neat rows." Another district leader stated that the initial money is good to put systems in place and give them a good "shot in the arm," but she felt the money was always intended to be short-term, somewhat as a pilot, and should lead to programs and activities that could be sustained. For example, she said that even if the parent ombudsman positions have been cut, the parent involvement and skills gained by parents should be sustainable over the next few years; that the system and approaches had to result in better capacity and sustainability.

VIEW FROM SCHOOLS

Several turnaround leaders I met had been approached by district leaders at a national leadership convention, likely because they had a certain kind of drive and confidence that made them stand out among other principals. Take William Wade, who was tapped in 2011–12 to lead turnaround efforts at Martin Luther King Promise Academy High School after showing success at increasing test scores at Vaux Promise Academy High School. Wade came to Philadelphia from Atlanta Public Schools, where he was assistant principal of a very large high school and in charge of its burgeoning ninth-grade student class. He enjoyed his work in Atlanta but felt the district was focusing more on the state test rather than what he felt was "good" instruction. He was recruited to Philadelphia at a national conference and found himself intrigued by the challenge of turning around a chronically low-performing school.

When Wade came to his school he found "a community that had opted out. The adults didn't believe in the school, and the kids saw the adults didn't believe in it." He said he saw some success in isolation but no common school culture. His first task was to have the staff interview for their positions.

He ended up keeping 27 percent of them, hired more skilled teachers to replace those he had let go (many of them new or first-year teachers), and focused on "setting a new mindset." As a Promise Academy, explained Wade, the school promises to give complete support to both teachers and students to be successful. Teachers in particular did not feel that before, so this model had those things in place. Supports for students included extended learning time, additional resources, and "tons" of field trips to expose and connect students to real-life situations. To support teachers, the school provided weekly professional development that aligned with their instructional needs and skill gaps. In other words, a teacher wasn't going to get training thrown at them just because it was required that they have "behavior management training." If they had already mastered a skill, they went to something that would help strengthen an area of need. These Friday professional development hours, called *power hours*, were informed by leaders doing regular walk-throughs to determine teacher strengths and needs. Sometimes the professional development included "instructional fairs," where teachers would walk through different areas to learn about a particular skill. Wade also used instructional specialists and teachers who excelled at a particular skill to do some training. Using strong teachers in this leadership role was important, he said, because it "empowered them in a way they hadn't been empowered before."

Regarding instruction, part of what had to change at Wade's school was to simply have teachers *teach*. From the data and his observations, students were off task, disengaged, and not learning. So he put in a uniform instructional model and taught teachers what he expected to see in their instruction, how to differentiate to address student needs, and how to use the state standards, and he made sure teachers understood how to individualize instruction. Wade recalled that training his staff on instruction the first year was easier, because he had almost all new teachers; not as many veteran teachers had signed up to teach at Promise Academies. After the second year, many of those teachers were lost to layoffs. Now Wade is less optimistic about his ability to help remold instruction with veteran teachers.

Research on strong turnaround leaders and practitioners is adamant that it takes a different and unique type of person to come into a school with a long history of a culture of failure and defeat and turn it around. Revealing his passion for the work, Wade talked about "storming" the classrooms and being present (not in a negative attacking manner but more in volume and purposeful urgency). It is important to note that Wade does not see himself as someone coming in to do magic like the heroic principal we often read about, where school success lies in the actions of one person; rather, he sees himself as putting systems into place. Wade describes the climate change process in his first school: "We had to empower the staff; it was a collaborative effort. Not just a principal standing up, arms folded, looking mad. It was a collaborative effort to change the climate, and even the young people bought into it. They saw us supporting them a lot differently than they had seen before."

Another concrete signal of a climate change was institutionalizing dress codes for school staff and uniforms for students. Wade felt these made a difference in attitude throughout the building, raised student confidence and increased staff professionalism, so dress codes were implemented along with higher expectations for conduct for the school. The school came off of the "persistently dangerous" list for violent incidents for the first time in six years. For the 2010–11 school year, it was down to fewer than five violent incidents.

Changing the attitude of the community and parents (and attitude *about* parents) was also an important part of Wade's (and the district's) turnaround strategy. To create a mutual connection between the school and community, the Promise Academies also focus on service learning projects that are planned and executed by the students. Examples include having seniors make up Thanksgiving baskets for families and managing a toy drive to give Christmas gifts to kids in the community. The community seemed to appreciate and respond to those activities. Students also learned a lot in planning the projects and felt empowered. Other activities included back-to-school block parties with a red carpet and a jazz band, providing an open-question platform weekly for parents called "coffee with the principal," and making sure teachers contacted parents regularly with positive calls as much as possible. The jazz band and red carpet were a "hook," said Wade, but really he wanted parents to come in and learn about the instructional model and begin to understand how to support their children's education at home.

During his first year before the block party, Wade described doing a school community walk-through: "We just stormed the community and flooded them with information, with the entire instructional team out with students dressed alike." Wade said the community had never seen this before, and once he had their attention he made sure he kept it by opening up the school, which apparently worked. Before Wade arrived, parent back-to-school night had yielded a total of thirty parents over the last three years. After the efforts of Wade, his team, and his students, that first red-carpet block party brought in 370 parents in just one night.

Wade was clear that this initial success was just the beginning: "It's my job as a leader to let them [the staff] know that momentum cannot be sustained on its own. You have to continue to push the momentum, the upswing of positive growth of the school." He and the staff kept up the momentum by ensuring that parents were at the table and that staff used the support model and interventions in place for students. He wanted everyone to know that they were accountable, that they were not allowed to fail a student without documenting all the interventions attempted, and that the parents and/or a case worker was present and involved in the process.

Despite movies like *Dangerous Minds*, we all know that students aren't going to suddenly morph from fighting in the hallways, sleeping in class, and threatening teachers to become enthusiastic model students. It takes continuous efforts to understand student strengths, weaknesses, and motivation. Wade said his school worked on changing student attitudes by understanding that they are "horrible decision makers," and that staff members are competing with video games and the fast pace of the information age. Thus Wade made sure that the staff were "loud and up front about their intentions" to teach students, and they put an incentive program (Cougar Cash) where students could earn rewards like t-shirts or even trips to New York. Once the systems were in place and students got the hang of the routine and experienced success, Wade said they didn't seem to need the Cougar Cash, because they were doing what was expected more as a norm.

After two years, Wade's school improved and was just a hair away from making AYP; he believes it will make it the next year. Although he will be moving on in 2011–12 to apply his turnaround skills to a larger high school (King), he was involved in

110

the selection of his successor, who he thinks will do very well in maintaining the systems put into place.

CONCLUSION

Philadelphia implemented a far-reaching and bold turn-around strategy that yielded some impressive gains for their first year. While the district has many great examples of how they changed the conditions and quality of education in many schools for many students, many of its leaders had a tough road to get there. The politics in this district seem almost in-surmountable—a board driven by the governor and mayor, a union that appears to function solely for adults, often at the expense of students in need of effective teachers, and a district left for now without a leader to help advocate for and continue to drive their improvement strategy. On the bright side, Arlene Ackerman might have found a way to mitigate so many internal and external challenges by creating a strong band of accountability from the community through parents.

5

⟡

DENVER PUBLIC SCHOOLS

Noteworthy practice area: Implementing an innovative regional approach with unique charter school partnerships.

Chapter Highlights

- Diverse school options
- Data-driven, strong performance management
- Innovative school models, particularly charter partnerships
- Regional approach

BACKGROUND

Denver Public Schools (DPS) is a relatively large and diverse district, with 162 schools serving 80,000 students, of which 72.4 percent are on free and reduced-price school lunch, 19.8 percent are White, 58.4 percent Hispanic, 14.6 percent African American, 3.3 percent Asian, and 0.7 percent Native American.[1] There are also a number of second-language speakers in the district, the top five languages being Spanish, Vietnamese, Arabic, Russian, and Somali. The district serves 31 percent of its students as English language learners (ELLs). DPS has been in the spotlight for a number of years for its innovative approaches, the most well-known being ProComp, a cutting-edge compensation system that links teacher pay to the district's instructional mission.[2] While the district had been doing some turnaround work before 2009 when Tom Boasberg became superintendent, the turnaround strategy now is bigger in scope and complexity.

TURNAROUND STRATEGY

Before 2009, Denver's approach to low-performing schools was primarily marked by numerous school closures due to decreasing enrollments and poor performance. In 2009, the district embarked on a longer-term, more ambitious district-level turnaround plan that has seen successes as well as bumps along the road from opponents of the plan. The first year of the new turnaround strategy, 2009, was mostly dedicated to building and gaining buy-in for the district 2010 strategic plan and putting together the structures to implement the plan. Those structures included fine-tuning the school accountability system, creating a decision-making structure to identify schools and the type of intervention they needed, improving community engagement, and making instructional improvements.

Figure 5.1 illustrates the theory of action outlined in the 2010 strategic plan, called the 2010 Denver Plan, that is applied to the district's entire work, including turnaround schools. The illustration shows that all strategies point to the student, who is affected by the instructional core. The three main pillars of the work are found in the yellow circle: (1) "great people" working inside the district, (2) family and community engagement, and (3) strategic management of financial resources. All three of the main pillars support teachers and principals in their daily work with students. The culture embedded within the process

FIGURE 5.1

2010 Denver Plan

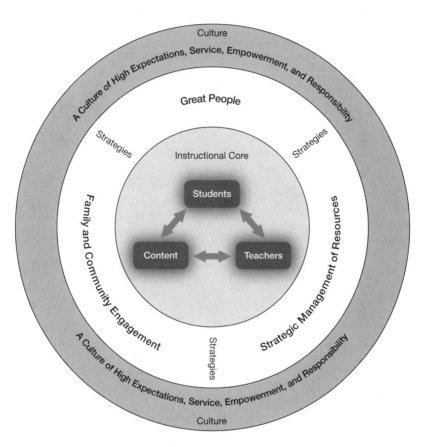

Source: Used with permission from Denver Public Schools.

is illustrated on the outside rim and consists of high expectations, service empowerment, and responsibility.

To improve accountability, DPS developed a system that would provide better information about school and district performance by including measures beyond the state test and the federal measurement Adequate Yearly Progress (AYP). To capture a school's progress over multiple years, DPS developed the School Performance Framework (SPF), which has since become a key tool in guiding decisions made within the district. The SPF has been updated several times since its inception in 2008 in order to assess the effectiveness of schools as accurately as possible. Indicators used in the 2011 SPF include:

1. Student progress over time—Growth
2. Student achievement—Status (e.g., percent proficient or above)
3. Postsecondary readiness—Growth
4. Postsecondary readiness—Status (e.g., on-time graduation rates)
5. Student engagement and satisfaction (attendance and satisfaction survey data)
6. Re-enrollment
7. Parent satisfaction

Each year in September, the SPF provides scorecards with four overall school ratings: Distinguished, Meets Expectations, Accredited on Watch, and Accredited on Probation. Within the indicators, scores are color coded as follows: Exceeds Standards (blue), Meets Standards (green), Approaching Standard (yellow), and Does Not Meet Standard (red). The color coding has provided DPS with an easily recognizable representation of performance that seems to be universally understood across the district.

Table 5.1 illustrates how the SPF provides an easy-to-read visual of how schools measure over time. In the third year, 2010, six out of seven red schools moved up to the yellow band, with one moving from high red up to blue.

TABLE 5.1

School performance framework: How schools are measured over time

School	2008–09	2009–10	2010–11
Gilpin Montessori	32	36	45
Greenlee ES	22	24	41
Lake International	23 (Lake)	36 (Lake)	45
Lake MS	23	36	50
West Denver Prep	23 (Lake)	36 (Lake)	90
North HS	23	36	43
Montbello HS	40	31	40
Noel MS	30	27	28

Note: ES = elementary school; MS = middle school; HS = high school.

■ Exceeds standards (blue);
☐ Meets standards (green);
▨ Approaching standards (yellow);
☐ Does not meet standard (red).

Source: Used with permission from Denver Public Schools.

As a part of their overall performance management system, all schools in DPS undergo a review by instructional leaders using the SPF. The turnaround process in DPS begins when a school receives a red rating. DPS's Office of School Turnaround director explained that a red rating does not automatically put a school in turnaround, but it does signal that the school needs some targeted assistance informed by an external diagnostic review, several of which have been lead by Cambridge Education.[3] After the review, if the school is identified for turnaround (meaning any of the four U.S. Department of Education models—turnaround, restart, school closure, or

117

transformation; see chapter 1), a stakeholder group is engaged to discuss turnaround strategies. Around October or November, the feedback is considered, and the board of education selects one of the four models to pursue.

After a school is identified for improvement, the school turnaround leaders work with the school to develop a plan. The school is expected to implement the plan with fidelity, and the school turnaround district leaders monitor the implementation as well as progress being made on increasing student achievement. The plans themselves are designed around three key levers: (1) instructional structures, systems, and processes; (2) human capital development; and (3) community involvement and engagement. These levers are discussed in detail later in the chapter in the Curriculum and Instruction, Human Capital, and Culture and Climate sections.

In addition to these three levers, the DPS board has identified additional drivers of the district's work: the belief that teaching and learning are the top priority; adult accountability matters; choice, collaboration, and innovation are key to twenty-first-century success; and parent, family, and community engagement are essential elements of quality education.

Choice and community engagement are important facets of DPS's turnaround approach. Underlying the philosophy of choice is some amount of competition, as students have a range of choices from which to select for their secondary schools. Superintendent Tom Boasberg asserts that choice is very important for empowering families, increasing their commitment to their school, and keeping a connection between parents and the school and between the kids and the school and their school peers. To create the choice model, students can pick from middle and high schools within a region close to their home. There is no default choice; they must select their school. The Office of Choice and Enrollment Services (OCES) coordinates the activities associated with getting students and schools matched. In early fall, students and families can attend a Middle and High School Expo to visit with principals, teachers, and students from traditional, charter, and magnet schools. Additionally, a lot of communication goes out to communities marketing the various school options.

An additional strategy to increase engagement and school cohesiveness is to shrink the size of some schools to form a coherent strong culture and foster strong relationships. Thus, some downsized or right-sized schools (because of enrollment attrition) share their building with a high-performing charter school. This strategy has been particularly useful in attracting students back to neighborhoods where gentrification has created a diverse mix of poverty and wealth.

According to Boasberg, Denver has a strong relationship with charters, and the district welcomes partnerships with high-quality charter schools. He describes DPS's relationship with charters as being very reciprocal and having "the same opportunities as the district-run schools." One could see how this could be a win/win situation, particularly for charter schools, which often face different funding challenges from those faced by other schools, particularly around facilities. Through this partnership, charters have the same access and level of funding for facilities, food service, and transportation, for example. "They also have the same equity in responsibility," Boasberg points out, explaining that the charters are able to share facilities, buses, and sports teams as long as they commit to work with all students, including gifted, struggling, and special needs students. He emphasizes that the charters are public schools that equally strive to serve the unique needs of all students in the district; charter schools have the same opportunities to serve all students while carrying the same obligation to ensure high-quality, standards-based academic programs. Accordingly, the focus on outcomes for all schools in Denver has helped the state close down many poor charter programs so that they may be replaced by stronger ones.

In addition to traditional, charter, and magnet schools, schools in Colorado can also apply for what is called *innovation status*. Made possible by the state's Innovation Schools Act of 2008, this status provides schools with autonomy and flexibility in academic and operational decision making, or as several administrators put it, "time, people, and money." The biggest advantage to this model is that schools and districts can gain waivers from state laws and collective-bargaining agreements. This model works particularly well for turning around low-performing schools because it allows them to extend the day or the year and have greater flexibility with human capital and instructional strategies. Currently DPS has nineteen innovative schools, which will be discussed further below.

Implementing the Strategy

While Denver had identified its lowest-performing schools around 2009, the district did not receive SIG funds until June 2010. The $14 million awarded to DPS was provided to address performance in eleven eligible schools. Of those, three were slated for closure and two were already undergoing turnaround. That left a total of six, depending on how you count them: three secondary schools for transformation, two elementary turnarounds, and one middle school to be split into two schools—one for restart and the other for turnaround. Other schools were targeted for reforms, and several new schools were planned and funded from additional outside resources.

The six SIG-funded schools were provided with additional funding and extra supports, including extended learning time, support from the Center for Data-Driven Reform in Education, deans of instruction to assist with professional development, weekly meetings for professional learning communities (PLCs), principal coaching, communication specialists to market and communicate new school efforts, and participation in district's new teacher evaluation pilot.

One of the unique features of the DPS turnaround work is its piloting of two regional turnaround strategies during the 2011–12 school year. The presence of a regional view of school performance becomes very evident when you ask anyone in DPS about school turnaround. In our interviews, the director of turnaround often swiveled her computer around to show me the regional map with SPF color-coding. A giant version of the same map is found in the main hallway of the DPS administrative building. Additionally, I found a video online of Boasberg making a presentation to parents within a region, drawing a big square in the air with his arms to represent the regions.

It is likely that this regional view is prompted by the clustering of "red schools" (the lowest-performance band) in two distinct regions: West Denver and the Far Northeast. As a result, both regions have been targeted for an aligned regional turnaround strategy, where they have been formed into networks that act somewhat like mini-districts. The West Denver Network Schools (WDNS) comprise five federally funded schools, with three additional schools in the Lincoln Collaborative and two that are undergoing transformation. The Far Northeast (FNE) region represents a larger regional strategy led by the

Denver Summit School Network (DSSN). DSSN's goal is to increase academic performance and provide more high-quality options to the region, which is characterized by high poverty and geographical isolation. According to the district website and interviewees, the DSSN was created by the district and leaders in the region who felt that change was needed. To achieve their vision, all schools in the DSSN have innovation status so that they can provide a longer school day and school year and daily small-group tutoring for students and have more autonomy over personnel strategies.

Another important feature of the regional strategies involved dedicating communications resources to build relationships; communications specialists were to actively inform parents about their choices and help "rebrand" schools to move away from their previous poor reputations. Several principals in FNE schools mentioned how helpful it was to have communications assistance for developing new logos and websites and marketing their schools to increase enrollment and attract more students from the neighborhood. The SIG finance office also remarked that the communications specialists seemed to have a very high return on investment (ROI) within the SIG grant: "Communications is one of the smallest items in our SIG grant, but the ROI is huge. We can invest 15K in communications, get twenty more kids, and gain . . . $100K for the district; it's terrific."

The DSSN is headed by Allen Smith, who came to the position in the 2010–11 school year as a leader who has been in the spotlight off and on for his success in turning around schools. Having previously done very difficult turnaround work virtually by himself, Smith insisted that the regional turnaround work be organized with a team effort and external partners because, as he said, "Turnaround is not for the faint of heart. It takes time. You know it will be hard, but it takes hard too a new level. The relationships, the pushback, it's very, very difficult."

When the opportunity came up for Smith to lead the FNE work, he decided, "If I'm going to do this, I have to be really smart and intentional about the systems I create. To do that, you have to have dedicated support and partners." Part of being organized as a network for the regional strategy meant functioning like a mini central office. Smith spends his time monitoring schools daily, and he has his own department representatives from human resources and payroll. Additionally, the district partnered with the Blueprint Schools Network (Blueprint) to help with the work and told principals and teachers that they were to be empowered and function like "co-directors." Having these positions made sense logistically, because the FNE is relatively far away from the DPS central office. However, Smith felt it was also important to have dedicated people right in the region to focus solely on their turnaround work. West Denver is now set up with similar positions and support.

HUMAN CAPITAL

As mentioned earlier, DPS sees people as the most important resource for driving student outcomes. Strategies outlined in the 2010 Denver Plan around talent management include:

- Recruiting the best teachers and principals
- Empowering and retaining effective educators
- Creating meaningful recognition systems, advancement opportunities, and rewards for driving student achievement

- Recruiting, retaining, and rewarding outstanding staff to support teachers' and principals' work
- Replacing low-performing employees who fail to meet expectations

Some of DPS's most interesting work falls under the third and fourth items above. DPS has long been recognized for its innovative compensation system, ProComp, which links teacher pay to student performance and other district priorities. ProComp has been in place for five years as a bargained agreement between the Denver Classroom Teachers Association (DCTA) and the district, funded by a voter-approved mill levy.[4] The more innovative features of the system include linking compensation to student growth data, providing additional compensation for hard-to-staff positions and flattening the pay scale by providing more money to early-career teachers.

One way the district is seeking to achieve the 2010 Denver Plan strategies is through elevating the teaching profession through its Empowering Excellent Educators efforts. The district is committed to rewarding and retaining teachers by providing recognition and rewards for good work as well as leadership opportunities and training supports. For recruiting, the district employs multiple pathways to teaching, which include a Denver Teacher Residency and using early hiring cycles to get the jump on competing for teachers. For evaluation, DPS aims to use multiple measures, and is piloting a new evaluation and feedback system in the 2011–12 school year called Leading Effective Academic Practice (LEAP). LEAP provides teachers with feedback on their instruction through multiple measures, including principal observation data, peer observation data, student perception data, an assessment of professionalism, and, eventually, student growth data. LEAP will move DPS evaluation from a historically binary system to a differentiated system with four levels of effectiveness—Not Meeting, Approaching, Effective, and Distinguished.

LEAP is grounded in the DPS Framework for Effective Teaching, which currently includes what DPS calls *onstage domains* (learning environment and instruction) and will include an *offstage domain* (professionalism). Data from each of the multiple measures is mapped to a competency area in the framework, which helps principals and teachers better understand performance strengths and weakness.

The framework also connects with an online professional development system. Every teacher sets two goals each year—a schoolwide area of focus and an individual area of focus. The entire professional development system is set up to align with the framework and provide multiple training resources. If a teacher is working on standards-based instruction, for example, there are over 140 online and offline resources to choose from. For the 2011–12 year, 94 percent of DPS's schools voted to participate in the LEAP pilot.

DPS was one of eight districts to receive funding to participate in a national research project also being implemented by Charlotte-Mecklenburg Schools: the Measuring Effective Teachers project. MET did not come up in any of the interviews I conducted, which may simply be because it was not included as a direct question; however, a central office leader mentioned in a follow-up interview that MET will inform the DPS Framework and the LEAP design.

CURRICULUM AND INSTRUCTION

Focusing on the instructional core is also a major component of the 2010 Denver Plan. According to the district website, improving the instructional core means that "teaching, schools, and systems are well organized to provide consistent, high-quality instruction that engages and challenges all students in acquiring skills, strategies and knowledge for the twenty-first century."[5] The activities under this goal include:

- Creating conditions to support principal and teacher effectiveness
- Ensuring that all students, including English language learners, gifted students, and students with disabilities, have access to rigorous standards-based curricula and assessments
- Providing coordinated and comprehensive support systems for students
- Using data and best practices to evaluate and improve instructional programs

The 2010 Denver Plan outlines numerous activities implemented during the 2010–11 year to improve instruction. Many of the strategies listed above are similar to those described by the five Broad Prize Winners highlighted in *Reform to Scale*, and are activities that have improved instruction in many districts. The practices I see as being particularly good include backward-mapping the curriculum from college to career readiness down the grade-level pipeline, setting performance targets at critical junctions, developing planning and pacing guides based on state standards, developing classroom "look-fors" and best practice documents to be shared, developing benchmark assessments on core subjects, implementing a district-wide response to instruction model, and creating principal professional development in literacy and mathematics instructional leadership.[6]

PERFORMANCE MANAGEMENT

The SPF is a major component of DPS's performance management system. The district is extremely data driven, as evidenced by the visible use of data by district and school leaders and teachers. Board presentations from the past two years contain pages of detailed data on almost everything, including student counts, achievement, demographic maps, seat counts, and gap analyses.

Performance management is a significant focus of the 2010 Denver Plan, which explicitly outlines a strategy to implement a continuous improvement process informed by data and best practices. The plan describes what continuous improvement looks like at all levels and schools also have separate teacher and administrator portals designed as one-stop shops to access all student data, standards-aligned curriculum, and resources for core content. At the district level, DPS is working to align evaluation and is continuously reviewing the effectiveness of programs, curriculum, professional development, and school design structures. For the turnaround schools, performance management is seen as a key lever for quickly identifying problems and coming up with appropriate interventions. This means using the SPF as well as using qualitative diagnostic processes to identify root causes of issues.

CLIMATE AND CULTURE

Culture and outreach are referenced repeatedly throughout the 2010 Denver Plan and were frequently mentioned in interviews. DPS works hard to ensure that district and school personnel foster and support a culture of mutual respect and high expectations. The fact that many struggling schools are beginning to move up the SPF color performance bands and have a different "look and feel" is testimony to the district's ability to make progress toward that goal.

The plan cites parent, family, and community engagement as being essential to quality educational systems. This area of DPS's work has been seen as crucial for connecting communities to schools and to the district. Like many big cities, Denver has experienced some middle-class flight out of some of its schools and even the district. To strengthen family engagement across the district, DPS established an Office of Parent Engagement and an Office of Community Engagement as a committed outreach resource.[7] Additionally, DPS has worked closely with community organizations like the DPS Foundation and the Denver Scholarship Foundation. Another important part of the engagement work has been to keep the community informed about DPS strategies and initiatives. To this end, the district has initiated an annual "State of the Schools" address to commence each September, hosted middle and high school expos, launched social networking sites, and created mechanisms for the community to send email to the superintendent.

Community outreach has been a major factor in the planning phases for DPS's turnaround effort. For example, when the FNE regional strategy was first discussed, the district held numerous community meetings to share data, propose strategies, and explain why some schools would be transformed, some closed, and some turned around. Additionally, the district invested considerable energy on communication strategies to build additional information tools like websites and marketing materials to help the schools build a new reputation through branding.

There was considerable community pushback around some of the turnaround work, as is typical when schools are being changed or closed. Many educators are frustrated that school communities often do not become engaged until reform is raised to the turnaround level. As an administrator in another district once lamented to me, "You can work hard to engage parents in a chronically failing school, and they don't show up. Then you begin talking about closing the school, and they show up in droves." Some leaders believe school closure creates community opposition because schools represent the fabric of a neighborhood, good or bad. The leader of the FNE region explained that even if the image of one school, Montbello, was not positive, the community around it was tightly knit and identified with the school. An Internet search on the rollout of the FNE plan yielded several videos (as with most media, likely containing cherry-picked scenes) depicting FNE community members decrying Montbello being changed from a transformation school to one being phased out and replaced by two different schools that would co-share the building: a 9–12 collegiate prep academy and a 6–12 Center for International Studies.

While several videos showed numerous protesters, others showed people asking the community to consider that they were receiving better options for their children. When asked about the opposition to the plan, one administrator stated, "The pushback is from defenders of the status quo who are unwilling to change even when terribly failing kids." This comment was associated with concern that teachers would lose their jobs once Montbello was phased out. The administrator continued, "It's a question of trying to protect adults' interests rather than putting kids' interests first." The Montbello case will be detailed shortly, but it's important to say that, after just two short months into the phasing in of the two new schools in fall 2011, Montbello, Collegiate Prep Academy, and Denver Center for International Studies again looks like a great place for students and for learning. Additionally, in October 2011, DPS reported its third consecutive year of enrollment increase; in October 2010, enrollment increased by three thousand students, and in 2011 there were an additional twenty-two hundred enrollments.

PARTNERSHIPS

I first selected Denver to be an example of a district-driven turnaround strategy that was executed without external partners. However, starting around 2010, the district began to engage with external partners for its ambitious turnaround work. Two administrators separately stated that during their first year implementing the turnaround work (in 2009), the district spent most of its time planning and putting basic structures in place, so it did not engage with any partners. Once the work was better defined, the district began to engage more partners for various purposes, with one of the main turnaround partners being Blueprint. Headed by well-known researchers like Roland Fryer Jr. (who evaluated Harlem Children's Zone), Blueprint focuses on five strategies: (1) excellence in leadership and instruction (2) increased instructional time (3) no-excuses school culture of high expectations, (4) frequent assessments to improve instruction, and (5) daily tutoring in critical growth areas.

All of the elements align very well with the 2010 Denver Plan and were frequently mentioned by turnaround school leaders. Allen Smith said that the partnership with Blueprint has been extremely important for obtaining objective data, having someone to bounce ideas off of, and having extra support to execute the difficult work.[8] Other partnerships that DPS has engaged in are in areas of critical need, such as Cambridge Education for school diagnostics, the National Center on Time and Learning to help with creative time management, and the Bill and Melinda Gates Foundation and the Walton Foundation. Additional partnerships mentioned earlier but still relevant are various charter organizations, community groups, and the DCTA.

CHALLENGES AND CHANGES

Interviews in DPS focused on the details of its turnaround work and tended not to reference political or other challenges, other than the fact that turnaround is hard and takes high levels of focus, intentionality, and time. However, research into DPS documents and news clips revealed some challenges and obstacles that appear to be continually present.

One potential challenge is that the board appears to have a consistent four/three divide, with four members supporting the DPS administration's turnaround work and three opposing it. While at some point it could cause issues for the district's reform plans, currently the majority is voting to support those plans. A bigger challenge is with the DCTA, which is currently suing DPS over the innovation schools. The suit, filed in June 2011, challenges the legality of the board's approval of the innovation applications earlier in 2011. DCTA's argument is that the required 60 percent vote of a school's faculty was not properly conducted, rendering eight of the ten innovation schools in FNE "unlawful."[9]

There are also places where the DCTA is mentioned in the 2010 Denver Plan, which may indicate areas of conflict. Most notably is a reference to the strategy of building "systems of mutual consent hiring, particularly in our highest-needs schools."[10] The section cites concern about high-need schools having to accept around one hundred forced teacher placements; it emphasizes the importance of allowing principals being able to hire appropriate staff for their schools, and advocates working collaboratively with DCTA and state policymakers on the issue.

VIEW FROM SCHOOLS

I had the opportunity to hear about and see several of the turnaround schools that really demonstrate what the work is all about. The first one was Montbello High School, the school referred to earlier that sits in the high-poverty, high-minority FNE area. Allen Smith, who leads the FNE turnaround work, explained that Montbello was originally modeled after a prison, basically because prison was the perceived next stop for its students. He said the teachers who worked in the school were the ones "on their last leg," and that community members felt that they were "the forgotten ones," or were different, like rebels. So, Smith explained, for thirty years the school had the reputation of being rough and tough and having the best fighters. It also went through twenty-seven principals in those thirty years.

Smith recounted that there were a lot of fights and two fatal stabbings, and despite the area's struggles, there was little political will to change it.

In 2004, Antwan Wilson, now a highly regarded central office leader, became the principal of Montbello and fought hard to change expectations and improve the school's performance. The work was particularly difficult, said Smith, as the community had so much entrenched negativity that it was difficult for an "outsider" like Wilson (who was from a different state) to fight. The campus improved under Wilson, however, and after three years he was asked to work in the central office. The school apparently did not stabilize after that time: it was selected in 2010 for transformation, then selected in 2011 to be phased out and replaced with two other schools.

In my interview with Smith, he said that I had to see Montbello, because this year it is "a completely different place." He told me that the new principal for the 2011–12 school year, Larry Irvin, had done a great job with the school thus far. Irvin, from inner-city Chicago, had a reputation as a steady leader able to turn around schools. Smith said that Irvin focused on respecting the teachers and students and did a good job making early wins by "plucking all the low-hanging fruit." In a recent tour of the school, Smith and district leaders were impressed with how well the building looked with "nice shiny floors" and students in classrooms—a school that "you could hardly tell was targeted for turnaround."

True to Smith's word, the building looked great, and the students were walking out of the building (it was near the end of the day) in a calm, organized manner not typical of high-energy high school students. Our first stop on the visit was to Collegiate Prep Academy (CPA), which currently is just serving grade 9. On our way to meet with CPA's principal, a ten-year veteran teacher who manages the intensive tutoring grabbed the turnaround director who was with me. Beaming, he showed us a clipboard: "Rebecca, you've got to see this. Look! This student just increased his reading score by 720 points!" Upon my asking what that meant, the teacher responded that it translated to moving from a second-grade reading level to almost grade-level.

Making our way down the gleaming hallways, we found the principal in an open area that looked more like business quarters than a principal's office. Speaking to the principal provided an opportunity to hear about the policy freedom the school has as one of the established innovation schools, one of the most important being the ability to hire, and, if necessary, fire staff. When teachers agree to join an innovation school, they agree to whatever hours and policies are implemented by the school, and it is their decision if they want to continue union membership. The teachers know they do not have a contract, and that they need to follow the policies set forth by the school.

Collegiate Prep is an early college high school; there is a heavy focus on raising instructional rigor, preparing students for college, and offering up to sixty hours of dual-credit courses for students to earn college hours free of charge. When describing the program, the principal and vice principal stated, "Students get a lot of support. No one is invisible, and there are plenty of different adults here for them to gravitate towards for help."

As we were talking, the tutor manager came in, still carrying around his data clipboard, showing everyone the latest results, particularly about the student he had mentioned earlier. I asked him what the student's reaction was upon seeing his score move up so dramatically. The tutor manager answered, "He cried." He explained that the student's father had been very ill, and that the youth had promised his father he would try to do better in school, so seeing the improvement meant a lot to him. Soon two female students came in to "hang out" with the principal, assistant principal, tutor manager and myself. There was a fair amount of giggling and talking about how hard the school is and questions about having a day where they do not have to wear their uniform. As I left, I heard one girl ask how she could get on the student council. The tutor followed me out and took me aside and said, "I want you to know, she was our second-most at-risk student. She used to miss school all the time and get into fights and in trouble almost daily." Now she is hanging out with school leaders and asking about student council.

My next stop was to interview Larry Irvin. Montbello's principal brought with him eleven years of experience as a teacher, an assistant principal, and then a principal at a large urban high school in Chicago. He came to Denver because he liked its feeder pattern turnaround approach and was excited about its new teacher evaluation system. He also felt he had something to offer with his experience and believed he could learn a lot himself.

When Irvin first walked up to the building at Montbello, he found mounds of trash piled up outside, and trash and food all over the hallways and in the cafeteria. He thought it was partly because lunch was held outside, and that perhaps the students had been intentionally acting out in reaction to the recent news of their school being phased out.

Irvin's first order of business was to build student and teacher morale. He observed that the seniors were sad and needed "a lot of TLC," so he planned a number of special activities for them. Following the same careful, intentional structure described in

135

one of my previous interviews with Allen Smith, Irvin got things organized, using "quick wins" first—for example, organizing the lunchroom and setting hallway and classroom routines. He also spent a lot of time working on building a positive culture with high expectations for staff and students, something that Smith had also cited as being a crucial first step. While Irvin was able to bring in some strong leaders and teachers to deliver a better instructional program, he also had the challenge of balancing the need to find the best talent with building up staff members with multiple credentials so that he could cover all subjects throughout the phase-out. When asked if the phase-out impacted his overall ability to attract and retain teachers, he acknowledged that it was a challenge to ask people to invest time in a school and a position that would disappear within three years, but that he was able to make headway by offering high-quality professional development. He noted that providing teachers with a strong background in data use, standards-based instruction, positive behavioral approaches, and strong instructional and organizational strategies made them very marketable for future positions.

As with other principals, I asked Irvin how he got students who had been known as "difficult" to listen to him and do small things like throw away their own trash to bigger things like pay attention in class. His response was that for the most part, the kids were really interested in pleasing the adults in the building and that the few "hardcore" students simply needed to have things repeated a few times, but in general they responded well, if not with surprise, to an adult being nonconfrontational and calm. Irvin and his staff work at applying what they call positive behavior strategies, and he describes his style as "applying relentless gentle pressure." Although

Irvin has only been leading Montbello for three months in its three-year walk to closure, he feels that the staff and students are making good progress.

I also had the opportunity to visit two schools in the West Denver turnaround network. Greenlee Elementary is a school that was "right-sized" because of declining enrollment and changed from a K–8 to a K–5 program. A strong principal and assistant principal were brought in, who in turn selected teachers to turn the school around. Behavioral and literacy coordinators, a coach for the principal, a community liaison, and a part-time social worker were also hired. Basically, Greenlee applied all the great interventions that are outlined in the 2010 Denver Plan. What brings that work to life is seeing the students quietly walking the halls and sitting in their classrooms attentively listening to the teachers. When I asked one third-grade teacher why she left her school to go to the second-worst-performing elementary in DPS, she said she wanted to work with a principal and staff she knew were good and committed to the students. She was very enthusiastic about her job, and she told how much she enjoyed working more closely with students and families by conducting home visits and going to family celebrations like her students' birthday parties.

Already after their first year last year, the teachers and staff members are seeing a difference in the students. One teacher attested that the work is easier this year, because her students are coming to her much better prepared for their grade level than the previous year. The staff who were interviewed also said that this second year seemed easier because all the groundwork of setting routines and fine-tuning logistics has been done, and they can focus more on instruction and on refining their systems.

137

I also visited the former Lake Middle School, which has been turned around to become Lake International and now shares the building with a restart, West Denver Prep (a charter school modeled like KIPP). This shared campus arrangement was a bit difficult to navigate with the SIG funds, as the DOE's opinion was initially that, since it was Lake Middle School that received the grant, the funds should go only to that school. As DPS's grant manager explained, DPS wanted to open a charter and turnaround a school. He felt it was within the boundaries of the grant, and the district wanted to apply two strategies. One was to use a CMO that had successfully yielded the highest middle school performance in the district; the other was to turn around the struggling International Baccalaureate Programme (IB). The grant manager further explained that another West Denver Prep school charter was capturing many neighborhood kids in DPS, signaling a demand for another, similar school. To meet that demand, DPS wanted to open such a school in the Lake neighborhood, while making good use of Lake's now partly unoccupied facility.

According to the principal at Lake International, Lake Middle School's International Baccalaureate (IB) Programme was not being correctly implemented, and the school was doing poorly in student achievement. As a result, its reputation suffered, and many students in that diverse and gentrifying neighborhood stopped choosing to attend the school.

The two Lake International teachers I interviewed had a great before-and-after view of the program, since both had previously taught in Lake Middle School. One teacher described her classroom in the original middle school as "isolated on the third floor," where she felt she could keep a safe and predictable environment for her students by closing the door to the chaos always occurring outside her classroom. The other added that teachers at that school often kept to themselves. In her words, "If you heard an incident going on in the classroom next door, maybe a fight, you ignored it. You minded your own business. It was everybody for themselves."

When I asked these teachers what Lake International is like now, the third-floor teacher told me that she now has her classroom door open and wants to share what she is doing with other teachers and observers. She said: "I know I'm valued, and my ideas are valued. I can help here, and I am mentoring other teachers who also desire to learn. I wish I had had that type of partner for myself earlier. Now I wake up in the morning feeling confident and stronger with a personal desire to see the school grow."

Teachers in Lake International are now implementing the IB program as intended and are using data on a daily basis to drive instructional decisions. They regularly share instructional strategies and observe each other teaching. The school has begun holding a regular student advisory to help students monitor their progress, and students are connecting with their teachers. Overall, students receive more clarity about what is expected of them, and the energy in the building, according to teachers and certainly observed by me, is positive.

CONCLUSION

There is a lot of positive work going on in Denver that is innovative as well as effective. The district's turnaround work is driven by a very thoughtful and well-laid-out strategic plan that drives the work across the district. DPS is not only implementing its turnaround systemically with district support, but is also attempting two large, ambitious, regional turnaround approaches. While the district has some challenges that could potentially hinder some of its work, it also has much in its favor to support it—talented leaders and teachers, a great comprehensive plan and approach, strong relationships with charters, tolerance for innovation and thinking outside the box, and schools that are already showing positive gains after just a few years of this iteration of work.

6

SACRAMENTO CITY UNIFIED
SCHOOL DISTRICT

*Noteworthy practice area: Connecting data inquiry to
instruction. Analyzed student work to better understand
how to yield high-quality instructional products.*

Chapter Highlights
- Implemented turnaround work as small pilot of six schools due to budget issues.
- Used small-scale implementation to more closely examine variables that helped or hindered their work and emerged with many lessons learned.
- Used a data inquiry approach that organically became a springboard to improve the instructional core.
- Turnaround partner felt giving schools a "fresh start" and image was more successful than trying to change existing schools.

BACKGROUND

Sacramento City Unified School District (SCUSD) has seen steady growth over the past decade and is one of the largest ten school districts in California. The district serves approximately forty-four thousand students, with 0.8 percent Native American, 18.5 percent Asian, 16.3 percent African American, 36 percent Hispanic, 1.5 percent Hawaiian or Pacific Islander, 18.6 percent White, and 7.0 percent two or more races. Last year, 69 percent of the students were on the free or reduced-price lunch program, and the district expects the number this year to be higher because of the recession. There are approximately eighty-two schools, including a number of small neighborhood schools and several choice options, with one independent study K–12 school, five dependent and six independent charters, and several theme-based high schools.

Jonathan Raymond, who had served as the chief accountability officer (CAO) in Charlotte-Mecklenburg Schools from 2006 to 2009, became the SCUSD's superintendent in 2009. When he arrived, he found an uneven picture of performance—some good, some bad, with more "complacency" (meaning "good is good enough") than stellar performance. He also felt significant disconnect between the community and the schools, so he put together a team to begin to construct a new strategic plan to increase performance at the struggling schools, with community input as an integral part of the process.

Raymond also came into a state whose education system has been subjected to deep budget cuts, and his district is one of eighteen California distracts that were disqualified from the SIG grant.[1] (As a side note, Sacramento was the first place I have visited with very visible signs of the recession, although perhaps that speaks more to where I've traveled. There were many neighborhoods with restaurants and businesses that had closed down in the past year. The locals I asked agreed that Sacramento had been hit hard financially over the past few years.)

So, given the lack of available funds, Raymond said that his focus was to figure out, "How to take limited resources, make immediate impact on the worst schools, close gaps, and innovate." He decided that he and his team would identify a small number of those schools, including one that was identified in the state's bottom 5 percent schools, build a strategy for turning them around, and group them together as the superintendent's Priority Schools.

TURNAROUND STRATEGY

Some of the changes implemented at the six Priority Schools resulted from overall changes Raymond made when he took leadership of SCUSD. To organize his team, he created an "academic shop" by hiring a CAO, who focused on curriculum, professional development, and increasing skill and capacity in schools. There was also only one department overseeing schools, so he created an accountability department with three area superintendents who would provide day-to-day support and coaching and hold schools accountable for working on continuous improvement. Finally, he created a family and community engagement department and recruited someone from within the community to lead it. This department built up "a whole web of services," including a family and parents program and support services like health, nursing, and youth development. Finally, the buildings were given some much-needed attention. According to Raymond: "Finally, for the first time in twenty to thirty years, they were cleaned, painted, landscaped, and given extra resources. We wanted to take them from the bottom and make them a place where kids want to go to school. We want them to have the best leadership, best staff, best training, and the first week that'll happen. I told the principals, you'll be jealous of them, but you don't want to become one."

In addition to creating appropriate central office structures, Raymond and his cabinet also drafted the 2010–14 strategic plan in 2009, which codifies many of the changes described above. The plan is built upon three pillars: (1) career- and college ready students, (2) family and community engagement, and (3) organizational transformation. As with the other districts profiled in this book, many parts of Sacramento's strategic plan relate to implementing or supporting the Priority Schools' improvement process. The first pillar aims to clarify the instructional program, develop clear instructional expectations, and connect instruction to the "real world," including college and careers. It also addresses continuous learning for the adults in the system by training everyone in the system on using data inquiry. To monitor instruction, the plan puts growth measures into place for every subject and grade level, trains teachers on common assessments, and agrees to define what exemplary academic writing looks like.

Pillar 2 addresses engagement activities such as offering parent classes and workshops, creating welcoming school environments, establishing a family resource center at every school, training administrators and teachers on developing family partnerships, and creating community gardens as a project to bring together schools and community members. This pillar also addresses creating more partnerships with higher education institutions and with business and communities to enhance college and workforce readiness.

Pillar 3 has significant impact on the Priority Schools, because it addresses how to align people, create accountability, and create organizational structures that will result in aligned practices to better support continuous improvement across the district, and specifically in Priority Schools. The first item under that pillar states that Priority Schools will be "places of innovation to attack persistent under-performance and the achievement gap." Accountability and improvement strategies include alignment of school development and improvement plans, school-quality reviews, and the budget; creating a management process and data dashboard for the strategic plan; enhancing talent management processes, including performance evaluations for all staff members; and establishing strategies to recruit, train, internally develop, and retain personnel. The final portion of Pillar 3 establishes cultural and decision-making norms that focus on "what is best for children," creating school environments that are conducive to learning, and reorganizing central office to facilitate "collaboration, improve collective accountability and enhance the quality of teaching and student learning."[2]

The announcement of which schools had been selected as the Priority Schools hit the newspapers in mid-March of 2010. The six Priority Schools included three elementary schools, two middle schools, and one high school. Of those six, four had failed to meet AYP in English Language Arts and math for seven years, and two had failed to meet the standards for four years. The schools were not difficult to group together, as five of the six were connected through a feeder pattern and had similar demographics. The schools had seen only minimal gains, and in some cases performance had declined. A seventh school, a middle school, was added to the list the following year. Because the district had to start small, it saw the Priority Schools as "incubators of innovation" that could pilot research-based successful instructional strategies and curriculum to be replicated later in other schools in the district. In reality, the superintendent believes SCUSD has about forty-four schools in program improvement, so he is eager to learn from the Priority Schools so that the effective pieces can be scaled across the district.

The Priority Schools report directly to the chief academic officer and are given her full attention. Additionally, they receive extra resources and protection from central office so that "principals can do their work." The Priority School process began with the selection of new principals who had an established record of increasing student performance. District leaders felt that it was important to have strong leaders who knew the culture and the system and had the skills to improve student achievement and build a positive school climate. The principals were allowed to bring in some teachers, but that step did not appear to be as formalized as in CMS; SCUSD had union restrictions Raymond had not faced during his work in the CMS accountability office. However, the principals were allowed to bring in their own leadership team, and teachers were told that they could leave if they were not interested in the new initiative. Raymond stated, "But if they believed in it and chose to stay, they would have to work their tails off."

According to Raymond, some teachers stayed eagerly; some stayed, but apparently to see if perhaps "this, too, shall pass"; and a fair number left those schools. Principals were then told that they could design "their own dream schools" by looking at their data and deciding what things to focus on. They were allowed to select their curriculum and extend the instructional day if they felt it was needed. The Priority Schools were also provided with additional supports, like learning specialists, coaches, data teams, and a parent adviser.

Raymond wanted the process of designing the Priority Schools to be collaborative, so a visioning team from each school was formed—including community members as appropriate—that met various times during the year to design the school using a customized Data Inquiry process (described next) and culturally responsive teaching practices. When asked if the schools had the capacity to design their schools and make those decisions, he thought they did, but felt that the high schools had a tougher time at first, because they had more staff members that had been "entrenched there for some time," and the schools had been suffering from years of leadership turnover.

While this work was being formulated, the district engaged an external partner to assist with the performance improvement process, using the Data Inquiry strategy. Herring-Peniston, president of Transformation by Design, LLC, had experience in the past leading Charlotte through the Data Wise process with Elizabeth City, one of the developers of the Data Wise Improvement Process. Data Wise, developed by students and leaders at the Harvard Graduate School of Education along with school practitioners, consists of three big categories of work and eight steps. The *Prepare* category includes setting a culture that trusts data and values collaboration and building assessment literacy through common language. The *Inquire* category involves creating a data overview through standard reports and graphics, digging into student data to "identify learner-centered problems," and examining instruction and comparing student work to come to a shared understanding of "effective" instruction. The *Act* category involves developing an action plan to solve the "problems of practice," planning to assess progress of that plan, and then the final step, acting and assessing.[3] The Data Inquiry process was crafted by Transformation by Design to accommodate the design needs of SCUSD. Herring-Peniston and her team revised the Data Wise process to incorporate two additional steps: reflection and making changes based on what was learned. These additional steps were added to help the schools incorporate what they were learning into the overall design of their school. In other words, leadership teams reflected on what they have learned and then created a plan for how they were going to incorporate that learning into the school practice.

While much of the Data Inquiry process falls under performance management, it also touches on instruction, because it involves connecting data to actual student work and discussing how the product and instruction can improve. Because principals were able to select their own curriculum and instruction, Herring-Peniston found the Data Inquiry process to be an important tool to get to strategies that would improve the district's overall instructional core and the additional steps for documenting what was learned and incorporating it into practice to help principals think about the overall design of their schools. Both of these approaches will be addressed further in the Curriculum and Instruction and Performance Management sections later in this chapter.

Herring-Peniston and her team worked in August 2009 on training the Priority School teams on the Data Inquiry process and helped them analyze their data to build their areas of focus. Some teams chose to focus on balanced literacy, tweaked the schedule to accommodate large instructional blocks, and engaged with a local university to train them on how to infuse writing across all subjects. Another school chose to focus on project-based learning and had students work in focus groups and complete projects together that related to topics and activities that occurred in their daily lives. Here is a thousand-foot picture of how the Year 1 work rolled out:

- District identified a principal.
- Principal built a team.
- Data inquiry teams, organizational teams, and core group were identified in each school and received Data Wise training.
- Teams reviewed student work and identified where instruction could be strengthened.
- Teams built a plan based on what they found.
- Teams incorporated what they learned into aspects of their overall school design.

As Herring-Peniston described it, Data Inquiry was seen as the "big bucket" or umbrella, and under that was the instructional core, which involved defining high-quality student work, looking at "problems of practice," and narrowing down instruction into "a set of discrete tasks for kids." District and school leaders said that they could see a change in instruction and student products through the work, and the process was rolled out to the rest of the district. The difference between how the first six schools were designed versus how the seventh, Rosa Parks, was designed was that the instructional piece was built into the actual process for Rosa Parks, whereas in the first six it was introduced as an "add-on" after it became apparent that more structure around instruction was needed. A bigger difference with the Rosa Parks school was that it was designed from the ground up, not a transformation of an existing school. So the Rosa Parks team spent time talking about aspects of vision and culture and identified "tangible artifacts." They built new rituals and celebrations as a strategy to build a new culture and set milestones for ramping up instruction to focus on college and career readiness. The students' first major project was built around understanding the legacy of the new school and discussing how to set up a new culture. The first set of schools are now embarking upon design work based on what they have learned during year 1.

SCUSD leaders and their partner see the work in the first year as stabilizing the environment, setting the focus on instruction, and using data to narrow that focus during the school year. In the next year, they will continue to drill down more into instructional improvement and building a positive school culture. Jonathan Raymond stated that he saw the district's role as "setting the course and expectation, and providing the environment and resources—serving as a backbone for the work," adding that turnaround work will always conjure up pockets of resistance, and that it was the district's role to help offset that resistance. He felt that it was important to extend turnaround beyond the school to the district, board, and the community. Similarly, the CAO, Mary Shelton, stated that the district's role was to provide sources and support, as well as some specific things like the parent adviser, instructional coaches, fiscal resources, professional development, and common planning time. While she admitted it was sometimes a difficult balance to be sure to provide time to other schools as well, she stated that it was important that the Priority Schools literally be the district's first priority; if they really need something, they can "go to the head of the line."

HUMAN CAPITAL

Union contracts limited SCUSD's funds and flexibility in terms of human capital. The district's main focus on human capital was to train existing personnel, improve human capital strategies, and put strong leaders in turnaround schools. To strengthen the principal pipeline, as part of the third pillar in its strategic plan, SCUSD instituted the Transformative Leadership Academy to systemically develop leadership pathways for the district. The Academy, which is not yet completely developed, will have four components:

- *Emerging Leader Academy*: Targeted toward outstanding teachers with three to seven years of experience who are interested in serving as a principal or in other leadership positions.
- *Principal Preparation Academy*: For individuals who already have credentials to be a principal and have been identified as outstanding prospective principals.
- *Established Leaders Academy (to be developed)*: To provide transformational and adaptive leadership training and growth opportunities to veteran SCUSD principals with satisfactory performance. Each participant will receive one year of executive coaching.
- *Summer Academy (to be developed)*: Current SCUSD principals who are in need of an intense immersion experience to better hone their leadership and managerial skills. Each participant will receive one year of executive coaching.

The district did not seem to have issues with teacher supply; however, district leaders explained that they are bound by union contract regarding teacher placement. When asked about the union relationship, leadership indicated that district and union seemed to have done well working together to agree on the plans for the Priority Schools, and that problems did not arise until the news of spring (school year 2010–11) layoffs came about. The disagreement centered around the district's desire to protect the Priority School teachers from layoffs, since they had specific training pertaining to their schools. Initially, the district's request was met with great resistance by the union. The matter was settled when the administrative law judge who oversees layoff hearings made a ruling in the district's favor—a first for California regarding this type of layoff decision. As a result, the union could not lay off teachers whom the district could prove had specialized training related to their schools. To make the documentation process clear, the district trained those teachers earlier, and documented the differences in what they were offered, which was more specific, particularly in the Data Inquiry training process.

CURRICULUM AND INSTRUCTION

In some turnaround efforts, there is more clear information on how organizations and schools changed than on how instruction specifically changed. In SCUSD, it seems very evident that changing instruction is an important part of the improvement work across the entire district. To this end, the district followed several well-researched approaches. At the heart of their instructional process was studying Richard Elmore's work about changing the instructional core. Elmore explains that instruction involves the interaction between three elements: the student, the teacher, and the content. Within those structures, he provides seven principles of improvement. Most of those principles center on being specific about how any change in one area, say the instructional task (content), requires a change in the other two (teacher and student).[4] Two of Elmore's other principles—that task predicts performance and that the real accountability system is in the tasks students are asked to do— formulate much of the in-depth work teachers do in SCUSD on better defining instructional tasks and examining student work in collaborative groups.

In addition to Elmore's instructional principles, the district also trained teachers on using *culturally responsive curriculum*— an instructional approach that recognizes and respects different cultures; incorporates cultural information into the curriculum instead of as an add-on; relates new information to students' experiences; teaches the whole child and treats the classroom like a community; addresses various learning styles; and maintains high expectations for student success.

There is much evidence that instruction has changed in the six Priority Schools. Each school has completed an extensive reflection on a year's worth of data inquiry that was turned into an in-depth study and record of its past work. The study includes detailed observations from each principal and the teachers on student instruction and includes multiple samples of student work. A review of the work over time clearly reveals the increase in quality. At one school, teachers spoke about improvements students are making as a result of their better designing and guiding writing tasks. One self-report statement read: "The degree of structure was not present before but now has better organization. Students aren't afraid of the writing process anymore, and it's gotten more complex. They've gone from singular to multiple paragraph pieces. From telling to thinking."[5]

A summary across the six reports found that there were visible changes in instructional practices at all schools. Reported changes included how teachers used textbooks, how teachers worked together to investigate learner-centered problems, how to increase expectations for student work, defining criteria for writing assignments, and having specific plans on improving instructional practices. The report also cites evidence of the school practices impacting overall district practices, as the criteria schools developed around some instructional tasks has been used at other schools and in district training.

PERFORMANCE MANAGEMENT

The Data Inquiry process, which applied the Data Wise approach, was a major driver of performance improvement at the Priority Schools as well as in the district. While the Priority Schools received the most in-depth training in the process, the external partner also trained the non–Priority Schools. The other major tool used to differentiate supports provided to schools and monitor progress is the school quality review (SQR). The SQR is a qualitative and quantitative assessment with information gathered by school visits on six domains affecting the overall quality of a school: progress and student achievement; leadership, management, and accountability; quality of learning, teaching, and assessment; curriculum; school culture and personal development; and partnership with parents and the community. Each visit has a uniform structure and is conducted by a reviewer at Cambridge Education along with two or more of the school's instructional leaders. The team spends two days reviewing data, conducting interviews, and visiting classrooms. The result is that each of the domains is labeled from "needs intervention" to "exemplary." Each school receives a summarized report of the findings, and leaders use the reports to guide their continuous improvement process.

According to one board report, the SQR approach was seen as so valuable that the district has begun the process of developing a similar Community Review Process that will be coordinated by the Family and Community Engagement Office. Parents, community members, and principals will develop a rubric to pilot during the 2011–12 year.

Sacramento's vigilant focus on performance management and instruction appears to be working well thus far. Figure 6.1 shows that all six Priority Schools made gains in composite (math, ELA) 2010 Academic Performance Index (API) scores. The purpose of the API in California is to measure the year-over-year growth in

FIGURE 6.1

SCUSD Priority Schools API 2010–11

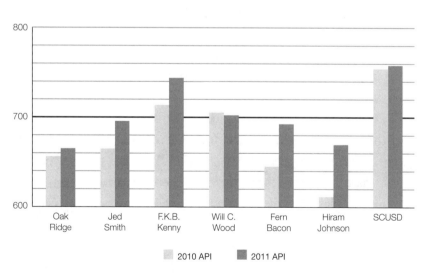

Source: Used with permission from Sacramento City Unified Public School District.

academic performance for California schools. The API summarizes a school's standardized test scores into a single number, which ranges from 200 to 1000. The statewide API goal is 800 for all schools; higher numbers generally indicate better performance on the tests.

CLIMATE AND CULTURE

According to SCUSD leaders, the culture has changed in the district from "complacency" and "good is good enough" to a desire and appreciation for excellence and working collaboratively to change culture and raise expectations for staff and students. Part of building that culture was improving the physical appearance of some of the buildings, and one Priority School got a completely fresh start and a new culture.

Not yet mentioned but a big part of the district's strategy is engaging parents and community members with schools. While each school decides which parent-engagement activities would be most helpful to its specific community, some examples of what has been implemented include dramatically increasing teacher home visits with parents and piloting a new parent education program, supported by Target, called Parents as Partners. Some activities led by the district's Family and Community Engagement department include a parent university that now has over eighty parent graduates, a parent/teacher home visit program, parent resource centers, and a parent connection portal. Parent documents are available to parents in English, Hmong, Chinese, Vietnamese, Spanish, and Russian; and the district has a dedicated Matriculation and Orientation Center to help families of children whose first language is not English with school and district enrollment and information.

Within all of these activities is the goal of connecting parents and their community to schools and spreading successful parent engagement practices across the district.

PARTNERSHIPS

As mentioned earlier, the district engaged with several partners for specific work, and then engaged an external partner, Rochelle Herring-Peniston from Transformation by Design, to help lead the process. Most partners engaged, such as Cambridge Education, had a reputation for doing high-quality, research-based work. Herring-Peniston's only challenge was guiding relatively complex work in a way that let the schools develop their own strategies yet gave them enough guidance so that they could understand the process. In addition to carefully steering the schools into building these skills themselves, Herring-Peniston was doing it while working from a distance and coming in for concentrated periods of time. Although she made seven school site visits to each school during the year and conducted three additional training sessions, she felt as though she was not providing them the time that they seemed to desire.

CHALLENGES AND CHANGES

Other than the obvious fiscal challenge, few big challenges were cited in the interviews I conducted. While the district might have wanted to address more schools with its improvement process, there seems to be some advantage to focusing on a small number of schools. The process was implemented relatively uniformly, and the district seemed to learn a lot of lessons from the approach because it was more easily able to identify

157

what was working and not working. Additionally, even though only seven schools were addressed in the district's focused improvement work, there was ample evidence that SCUSD was able to scale much of what it learned from the Priority Schools across the district.

Another challenge mentioned was working with the union to protect the Priority School teachers from seniority-based layoffs (however, as noted, the presiding judge ruled in favor of the district; an uncommon finding regarding layoffs in California). The district also had difficulty in getting creative with how it managed time and talent to create greater innovation and incentives within the schools.

Regarding the fiscal challenges, the district did not get a SIG grant but had some American Recovery and Reinvestment Act funds and used its Title I funds to support the rest of the Priority Schools' needs. SCUSD set aside a fair amount of money to improve their most struggling schools, because they felt those schools needed to be ramped up as a result of previous neglect. CAO Mary Shelton explained that the district tried to help schools use their dollars well by ensuring that principals understand the budgeting process and providing assistance to them as needed, including assigning a "budget technician" to help them with that process.

Perception of SIG and Turnaround

Regarding the SIG program, SCUSD leaders felt that closure was not a good option since a number of its schools are small neighborhood schools, and several leaders were not particular fans of charter schools. Overall the district felt that the grant provided too little flexibility to allow much creative innovation. One administrator thought that the two-year timeline outlined in SIG might be reasonable for some schools, but that high schools, being more difficult to change, would require five years rather than two.

VIEW FROM SCHOOLS

I had the opportunity to sit in on the first Priority School planning meeting in August 2011 with the Priority School principals. They began the year by reviewing their data, planning a board presentation, and then speaking to me about their turnaround experiences. To provide a school view, I'll outline some of their experiences by school: however, to keep the focus on their actual practices, I will not refer to them by name.

School 1: The principal's first priority was to change the culture, which she described when she first arrived as "having been toxic for a number of years." She was hired two days before school started, and inherited her staff. She focused primarily on students' time on academic tasks, looking at data, and making sure teachers were implementing good instruction. Apparently, the school had seen a lot of leadership turnover, so this principal said she was asked by a number of students, "Are you going to stay?" By the second year, she had gotten things put into place and running smoothly, and she has been pleased by her test scores, which are improving. She wants to keep that momentum, still feels a "sense of urgency," and says that while she is "humbly proud," she "still has a lot of work to do."

School 2: School 2 is a high school. The principal stated that his task of organizing and structuring the academic program is "compounded multiple times because teachers were entrenched and extremely reluctant to change. Thus he brought in several staff members he knew that could help impact the staff positively. This principal stated that his biggest hurdle was the mindset of the teachers and helping them raise their expectations for students. During the first year, student achievement increased significantly, and staff members were encouraged by their students' progress. The principal stated that he thought it was more difficult transforming an existing school because it requires taking apart a long-term culture. He felt starting a new school and creating a new culture would be easier.

School 3: The principal of this middle school said that her year was difficult, partly because she had no money to incentivize teachers to come to her school, which she felt made the work harder. She felt that the professional development she and her teachers received had "high-yield impact," but she also felt that the most valuable resource to her would be "one right Language Arts teacher." She also mentioned that a strong assistant principal is "worth their weight in gold."

School 4: This school's principal found that many teachers did not have a clear understanding of "what good instruction is," so he thought it important to work with them on taking lessons apart and making them more interesting. He observed that at times teachers would conduct very bland lessons from "scripted" texts, and "as long as the teacher didn't throw bricks, it was a success, but you saw numb kids not engaged in the learning." He emphasized that when teachers apply good innovative practices, suddenly the kids are excited, want to be there, and respond well to the idea that the adults believe in them.

School 5: School 5's principal said her school "flatlined" because she was the last one hired and the teachers were no longer there, so she had to do planning over the summer without staff or much support. Her school had a history of being tough, teachers who did not get along, and students who often engaged in fights and other negative behavior. She met with the students and with her school team, explained expectations for the school, and led several team-building activities. This principal brought stability to the school, and parents began to comment that they felt the school was a safer place for their children.

The schools and the district gained a lot of information from the detailed data inquiry reports done at each Priority School. Key findings across these six schools include:

- Data inquiry is difficult and likely will result in different approaches by different schools.
- There was widespread change in teacher practice.
- The district set the conditions to support the data inquiry process by putting common planning time into place and offering professional development in data inquiry.
- Student work improved as a result of the data inquiry process.
- Products from each school's inquiry process were used by other schools across the district.
- The schools have plans to take the inquiry process to the next level for the upcoming year.

Some of the individual lessons shared in the reports were interesting and are worth mentioning to illustrate the power

161

of connecting data inquiry to creating a culture that regularly collaborates to analyze and improve instruction. In one school that had struggled for years, the process prompted teachers to appreciate and request data and shifted their perception about students to a much more positive light. That school also found that teachers were only using about 15 percent of their ninety-minute block schedule time for instruction, so it changed the schedule and curriculum to segment out instructional time into forty-five minutes of actual teaching. In another school, when math teachers discovered the benefits of e-mailing student work to their department colleagues, they formalized the process as departmental "mini-cycles." For a mini-cycle, a department would analyze a learner-centered problem from benchmark assessments, identify the "problem of practice, "and then build an action plan. Another principal described how, when analyzing student writing samples, she and her team realized that the professional development the school was providing for teachers was insufficient to produce the type of tasks and student writing itwanted teachers to have students produce.

CONCLUSION

With limited funds and flexibility, SCUSD has moved the needle in its first six Priority Schools. The district had to start small, but ended up learning quite a lot about the improvement process, because it was more easily able to isolate which practices yielded the most leverage, and which ones become lessons of what not to do. One of the most interesting outcomes of the district's work was the ability to focus on instruction through the data inquiry process to the degree that student work, teacher instruction, and learning tasks were scrutinized on a regular basis as a means to improve instructional outcomes. The end result was a culture of collaboration and the desire to constantly improve and to spend time having honest discussions informed by data on how teachers and assignments can be leveraged to result in more rigor and higher expectations for students. An additional laudable outcome was the influence this work had on practices across all schools and the level of support provided by the district to the schools.

7

❦

LONG BEACH UNIFIED
SCHOOL DISTRICT

*Noteworthy practice area: Coherence and innovation.
As a high-functioning system, the district is well positioned
to pilot innovative approaches that can be easily
implemented and monitored.*

Chapter Highlights

- Provides an example of turnaround prevention.
- Implements innovative structures, like a sixth-grade academy.
- Uses implementation of performance improvement schools as a pilot for strategies that would work well districtwide.
- Exemplifies a high-functioning organization where most innovations and programs are likely to succeed.

BACKGROUND

Long Beach Unified School District (Long Beach) is the third-largest district in California, serving a diverse city where dozens of languages are spoken. It has approximately 87 schools and serves 84,000 students, of which 70 percent are low-income, 24 percent are English language learners (ELL), 17 percent African American, 52 percent Hispanic, 16 percent White, and 1 percent multiracial.

Long Beach has gained attention for a number of reasons. It is the 2003 winner of the prestigious Broad Prize for Urban Education, was one of the first U.S. public school districts to require school uniforms in grades K–8, and has been recognized in numerous publications for its improvement gains (including *Bringing School Reform to Scale*).[1] Long Beach also is making a mark as one of the only urban districts to have only two superintendents in two decades, the much-heralded urban leader Carl Cohn (1992–2002) and now Chris Steinhauser, who has filled the role since 2002.

I first selected Long Beach for this book because it was part of the California Collaborative on District Reform, and featured in a piece on district turnaround strategies, as was Sacramento. However, when I called Chris Steinhauser, he informed me that Long Beach has not had any schools fall onto California's "bottom 5 percent" list since 2009, and thus the district did not quite fit the criteria for this particular book on school turnaround. However, part of the premise of turnaround being approached at the district level is not only to see schools identified by the state as being in "improvement status" get off that list, but also to improve practices across all schools to prevent more schools from appearing on that list. Thus, Long Beach does, in a sense, have a "turnaround strategy" in the form of a school improvement strategy being applied to its most struggling schools.

Some existing elements in Long Beach's system should be explained before I outline the district's approach to their

166

struggling schools. It is because Long Beach is such a well-defined, focused, aligned, and data-driven system that almost any reform is bound to find success within the system. First, the district has suffered from little leadership churn, since it has had two stable, strategic leaders for twenty years. Stable leadership also means that reforms are kept in place and implemented over many years, as long as the data show they are working. Rather than moving from one education fad to another, the district spends time drilling down further, refining its practices, and tweaking where the data shows adjustment is necessary.

In 1992, Long Beach was hard hit when a major naval base shut down. In response to the worsened economy, the district embarked on building a stronger education foundation. Its approach was simple but effective: it raised expectations and image through school uniforms; ended social promotion so that students who had not mastered the content did not pass through grade levels; instituted a third-grade reading initiative to get students on grade level for reading by that grade; and did not allow eighth-graders with two or more Fs to go on to high school. So from the start, the district had a positive image, clear expectations, and attention to the K–12 pipeline so that students did not slip through the cracks academically.

The district is also known for doing things "the Long Beach Way"—a pragmatic process through which the district applies strategies and implements programs based on what works for the system. This can mean a practice may come from a teacher, or may come from the superintendent's office; the focus is on outcomes and implementing change to fit the existing system. In addition, instruction is viewed through a collaborative lens informed by data and clear expectations. The Long Beach Way has helped turn the district into a high-functioning system that has operationalized its vision of high standards by clearly defining expectations for teachers and students. Along with clarity comes the provision of a multitude of supports to ensure student success and continuous performance monitoring as an integral part of identifying supports for schools, teachers, and students. These elements brought together the system that was first recognized when it was awarded the Broad Prize in 2003, and then being named a Broad Prize finalist again from 2007 to 2009.

TURNAROUND STRATEGY

When asked what has kept Long Beach Schools off the state's corrective action list, Steinhauser explained that it was the district's systemic approach to school improvement. When one math teacher decided to reorder the math sequence one year, resulting in a huge leap for his students, that teacher became a math coach for the district and began to work with schools across the districts on his approach. "A lot of systems only do certain things in particular schools at certain levels," stated Steinhauser. When schools in his system do not meet expected performance targets, they receive differentiated supports and monitoring.

Long Beach has identified eight out of its twenty-two K–8 schools as being in "program improvement." Once they were identified, the district's strategy was to put these schools in a subgroup and have them function as *professional learning communities*, or PLCs. Additionally, to address a performance drop district leaders found between fifth and sixth grade, the district moved all sixth-graders from those eight schools—all two thousand of them—into a self-contained sixth-grade model. All those schools now have new English Language Arts (ELA) and math programs and new support structures, and their scores have "skyrocketed," according to Steinhauser. The PLCs have made improvements between 2010 and 2011, with most of the growth happening within the sixth grade, as illustrated by figure 7.1. While aggregate district scores are still higher in math and ELA, the sixth-graders at the PLC schools were only five percentage points behind the district in 2011.

Figures 7.2 and 7.3 illustrate that the seventh- and eighth-graders did not show as much growth as the sixth-graders; the seventh-graders in both PLC schools and districtwide showed little to no improvement in math between 2010 and 2011.

Overall, the results suggest that the interventions for the sixth-graders had a measurable impact on the PLC students

FIGURE 7.1

Grade 6 ELA and math, 2010–11, PLCs and district

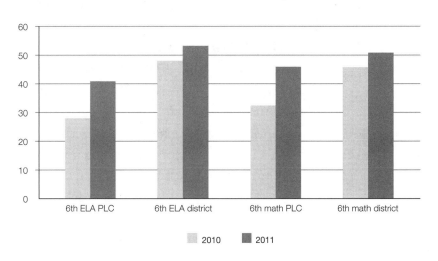

Source: Used with permission from Long Beach Unified School District.

FIGURE 7.2

Grade 7 ELA and math, 2010–11, PLCs and district

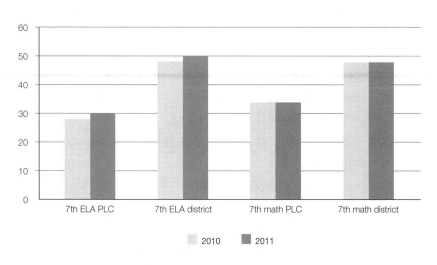

Source: Used with permission from Long Beach Unified School District.

over the last two years, and illustrate that these schools are improving overall, even if incrementally.

The sixth-grade academy marks a stride outside of the box for a large urban district. All students are contained in one building (or one-and-a-half) so that teachers have complete flexibility over the students "all day long." If they want to have a three-hour ELA class that integrates social studies and writing, they can do that. The day is not controlled by a bell, there is no passing period, students stay with the same teacher all day, and students go out for PE together so that teachers can meet weekly and plan. The academy also places the most struggling readers in a class with a handpicked teacher, a separate curriculum, and a 25:1 ratio; these students to basically do math and ELA all day long.

FIGURE 7.3

Grade 8 ELA and math, and Algebra I, 2010–11, PLCs and district

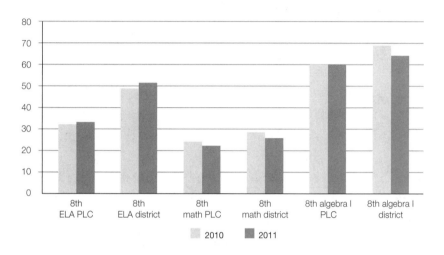

Source: Used with permission from Long Beach Unified School District.

Another practice implemented at the sixth-grade academy was to have teachers meet every quarter after they received their quarterly formative assessment results, regroup the students by level, and then split them up by strand. For example, a student struggling in fractions would work with one teacher for a few weeks, retest, and then move to another teacher who could address the next level in that strand. After a few weeks of regrouping, the students were tested again, and their proficiency numbers took off. Because of the success of this practice, it is being implemented across the district.

The above examples illustrate how Long Beach has used its intensive improvement work in a small number of schools, as Sacramento has done, as a pilot for approaches that could be used across the district. As Steinhauser puts it: "Our turnaround

171

work is not punitive. It's a sense of how we will all work to-gether, and we have these eight schools that become a Petri dish of education reform activities. The ones that worked well are re-fined and exported out to the main level of schools."

Overall, the success of the PLC schools has elevated the low-est-performing schools to a level they have never known be-fore—they are now being seen as leaders of reform efforts. When asked if the sixth-graders appear to be better prepared for the next grade levels, Steinhauser replied that not only were seventh- and eighth-grade teachers surprised by the incoming students' preparedness, they also are starting to look at adjust-ing the rigor of their own curriculum in response to these stu-dents' higher skill levels.

The PLCs are placed directly under the superintendent and are overseen by a director who is a researcher so that she can examine new tools, test them, and share them with principals at those schools. Three principals with strong track records for increasing student performance in middle school serve as coaches for the PLCs. In addition to coaches, the PLC admin-istrators have an assistant principal dedicated to performance management, participate in monthly PLC meetings, and re-ceive instructional coach feedback. Teachers also have instruc-tional coaches, as well as quarterly trainings, monthly support meetings, and individual coaching for the sixth grade.

HUMAN CAPITAL

PLC schools are led by strong principals with established re-cords of helping improve student achievement at their cam-puses. When asked about the union's impact on teacher place-ment, district leaders stated that principals have total authority to staff specialized positions, like an ELL teacher or a gifted and talented teacher. The other positions are filled by transfer and assignment, which are based on seniority (if no teacher chooses to take a PLC assignment, then a principal has authority to choose who will fill that position). To offset that practice, the district fills positions at PLC schools first, and no principal of a low-performing school will receive a teacher who has an evaluation of "less than proficient," which is a provision in the union contract.

In the course of the school interviews, one principal (Michael, who will be profiled later) voiced frustration at not being able to hire his own teachers. Rather than citing other external barriers to increasing student performance as some educators tend to do, this principal said with a great deal of confidence, "Anybody knows, if you get to hand-pick who [teachers] you want, there is no excuse for you not to be a distinguished school.[2] If I could do that, I would have guaranteed it." As it was, out of fourteen positions he had to fill one year, he was able to select only about seven, and only because they were special program positions.

The union contract does appear to differentiate its policy for low-performing schools. Were a principal to end up with a teacher who was not doing good work with students, Steinhauser stated that principals can document the issues, because Long Beach has historically taken the time to remove ineffective teachers. However, Long Beach does not have particular issues attracting high-quality teachers, partly because of its positive reputation, but also because of its unique partnership with California State University Long Beach (CSULB) and Long Beach City College. Working with other community and regional partners, Long Beach and its higher education partners represent a true P–16 partnership that has been functioning for years, as I learned in 2005 when conducting a sustainability study of past Broad Prize winners. Together, the systems have created a seamless pipeline from preK to graduate school by aligning academic standards, teaching methods, and student assessments. Once teachers leave one of these higher education institutions, they have a good grasp of the Long Beach Way.

As a result of this partnership, the CSULB teacher preparation program has changed in response to district feedback and the district curriculum has been adjusted according to CSULB input. For example, years ago the district worked with CSULB to strengthen students' narrative reading skills. The combined work of professors, teachers, and district leaders led to the development of twenty units of study focusing on high-interest, high-level nonfiction text, complete with a template for creating future units. The inclusion of district leaders on CSULB faulty search committees and the addition of a district evaluation of CSULB teacher graduates mark additional joint activities that have benefited both organizations. As a result, even if principals do not have full leverage to select their own teachers, they do appear to have a steady incoming pipeline of well-trained teachers.

CURRICULUM AND INSTRUCTION

As mentioned throughout the book, successful improvement processes must consider how well the curriculum is articulated in each grade level and through the preK–12 pipeline, monitor curriculum implementation, and connect the curriculum to instruction by reviewing data and student work. One of Long Beach's greatest advantages is that it has been refining those curriculum strategies at least since 2003. The district has established common academic language and clear instructional expectations throughout the instructional year by using curriculum pacing guides, and by monitoring curriculum implementation through frequent formative assessments and classroom walk-throughs. When a gap is found in the curriculum, or the units organized in the pacing guides are not working, midcourse corrections are made either by the district or through teachers, depending on where the best outcome can occur.

Walk-throughs also serve as a way to keep abreast of teacher needs. Once instructional issues are detected, a coach can better target work with individual teachers. The appearance of common instructional issues may result in a school or district's adjusting its professional development for teachers.

Instruction and student work are also closely monitored. If a group of students appears to have a need, schools will make short-term adjustments (such as dividing students into small groups by instructional needs and matching them with teachers whose strengths match those needs) or they will provide longer-term interventions (such as creating a self-contained school that has full academic flexibility like the sixth-grade academies). Whether short- or long-term, interventions are closely monitored, and they cease either because they are not working, they are continued and refined, or they are implemented to a larger scale if needed.

PERFORMANCE MANAGEMENT

During the 2003 Broad Prize site visit to Long Beach, district administrators described their student assessment and monitoring systems as "seamless." At that time, the district was already an exemplar of strong performance management, meaning it had access to numerous data sources to continuously ensure that leaders, teachers, and students were yielding strong student achievement and had the resources they needed. Data were used as a system of prevention, so that problems could be addressed systemically and early when they were small, rather than later when they required more intensive and likely out-of-school-interventions. Long Beach continues to refine what works and replace what does not; it is clear that after almost nine years, performance management has become a powerful asset in the district.

Teachers and administrators are easily able to input and access a variety of static and live data through Long Beach's intranet/Internet data system. Additionally, the district's new website interface, School Loop, provides a mechanism for various stakeholders to keep updated about district and school news, view data, and access the parent portal to monitor grades and homework.

Long Beach's sophisticated use of data has helped enhance instruction, support, and intervention across the district, particularly for the PLC schools working toward improvement. Data are used continuously to correctly place students in courses; monitor student, school, and cluster achievement; and better target support needs, such as how coaches can best be utilized. Additionally, reviewing data in stakeholder meetings at various levels is a common practice. These data management practices are a significant contributor to Long Beach's high-yield results, and have thus attracted the attention of other districts. High levels of transparency and accountability are achieved through the walk-throughs, unannounced superintendent visits, and quarterly superintendent data review meetings, where principals receive written feedback after each meeting.

CLIMATE AND CULTURE

The culture of Long Beach remains similar to what I found in 2003. The district is proud of its accomplishments; teachers and administrators work collaboratively in an environment of trust and focus continuously on raising expectations for staff and students. When I've asked at different times what national recognition has meant to them, most leaders and teachers say it has been great to get "a shot in the arm" of positive external recognition of their work. However, they know that they are not where they want to be with student achievement, and they have much work to do.

In the area of external relationships, the district has worked hard over the years to increase interactions and communications with families and the community. Since 2005 the district has had parent coordinators, hosted an annual Parents Institute, and presented information to parents on college-readiness, and has hosted events with local celebrities (Long Beach is near Los Angeles) to draw in a large crowd. The district appears to be doing some navigation to be sure that schools have effective leaders and teachers, and there appears to be a positive working relationship between the teachers' union and the district.

PARTNERSHIPS

When making the decision to "build or buy," Long Beach has always shown preference to "build." The district is not currently working with a specific external turnaround partner, and in general believes that its improvement work should be done as a part of its overall district strategies, instead of as an "add-on" or as a separate program by "those people" (Chris Steinhauser's summing up of prevailing perception from within the district regarding working with external partners). It is not that district leaders do not see a place or value for external partners for school improvement work. Rather, while they agree that many districts do not have the knowledge or capacity to do the hard work of school improvement to turn around on their own, Long Beach currently does.

Regarding stability, Steinhauser said, "It all goes back to culture, really. If I left tomorrow, the system will continue to improve, because it's part of the culture and is embedded. A new superintendent could not turn it upside down."

CHALLENGES AND CHANGES

While all districts experienced increased fiscal challenges after 2010, particularly in California, Long Beach found some ways to address those challenges, marking a departure from its traditional budgeting practices. To accomplish its plans with limited funds, the district switched from a decentralized to a centralized way to spend categorical funds. Steinhauser explained, "To achieve our desired outcomes, we needed to centralize those funds to ensure that the limited resources we have are being spent in the most efficient manner." Steinhauser estimated that the PLC schools this year cost roughly an additional $3 to $4 million. To pay for that, the district took money off the top of the Title I budget. That practice is allowed, said Steinhauser, through a Title I provision. The non-PLC schools were told that their money needed to be spent on activities outlined in the strategic plan to close the achievement gap.

Steinhauser pointed out that centralization of funds was a very different practice from when he was a Long Beach principal and was told, "Here are the goals that you need to meet; it's up to you how you do it." Now, he commented, "It's centralized, still with a lot of autonomy, but not on how you are going to spend these major resources." He further noted that school leaders were fine with the switch because they understood the equity issues and it was part of an agreed-upon strategic plan developed collaboratively with multiple stakeholders. In the end, Steinhauser observed, they had some interesting results. For example, the district has a goal to increase the number of students in Algebra I by 10 percent every year, and right now the number is at 55 percent. More support is needed for students who need remediation, so each school has set up an algebra development course out of its site budgets. "Some schools might not have chosen to do that on their own," said Steinhauser, but this time they did it because it was in the strategic plan. As a result, the algebra proficiency rate is about 68 percent, so the district is not only increasing the number of kids in algebra, it is doing so while holding their proficiency level. Thus, parents, teachers, and administrators are happy because they receive support systemwide.

There are some things the district has not been able to do because of limited resources. It would like to address more schools, and it does not have summer school for students who need remediation or acceleration. Steinhauser did have some advice on how to better utilize limited resources, including:

- Roll out programs like technology over a multiyear plan.
- Focus on instructional intervention during the school day.
- Align site-level plans to the district's strategic plan.
- Focus resource allocation by looking at data and aligning specific resources to fix problems based on data.

PERCEPTION OF SIG AND TURNAROUND

Long Beach does not use the term *turnaround*; rather, it refers to its efforts as *continuous improvement*. To ensure they meet their goals for all students, educators in Long Beach focus on subgroup data to accelerate growth and close achievement gaps. Regarding the SIG grant itself, Long Beach interviewees agreed that schools can make dramatic changes within the short timeline outlined in the grant, but not necessarily by following the four prescriptive models. Again, a medical metaphor was mentioned, highlighting the importance of the context of a school to the need for an individuated treatment for more serious diseases like cancer. "If I have cancer," said one leader, "the doctor may say, here, take this standard cocktail. Maybe it worked for 90 percent of the people, but you have to dissect my DNA, my cancer, and there might be some trial and error, but it is possible to find the right solution to fix my problem. We all have different DNA. It's the same with schools; each community is unique."

VIEW FROM SCHOOLS

Many of the PLC schools have been reconfigured to provide innovative programs that meet the needs of specific school communities. They are led by strong leaders, who are selected by the superintendent based on their proven track record in improving student achievement and school climate, as well as their ability to connect to and lead a school community. Many of these leaders were provided a good deal of autonomy in creating the programs they felt would best address their student needs. Two of those examples are illustrated next.

Marshall Academy of the Arts

Michael has started his second year as a PCL principal at Marshall Middle School. Previously he had led a high-performing school for ten years. When tapped to lead Marshall, he said, "I knew what parents wanted from the school, and I knew what the school needed, including a changed image and parent involvement." The board made a decision to reconstitute the school, and he was left to figure out how to change the school into a place where students wanted to learn and teachers wanted to teach. What was unique and different about Marshall was that it was in what was described as "a nice neighborhood" but had experienced significant flight of wealthier students to other schools. To ascertain what kind of school would draw students back, Michael researched schools in the area, conducted some surveys, and studied the schools that his school tended to feed into. He found that the high school nearest to his school had a popular visual arts program that was structured in small learning communities. Thinking that moving that model down to the Marshall was a good fit, he got permission to turn his feeder middle school into a magnet school that offered two electives for students in the arts, as well as a specialized gifted and talented program (GATE) and a college-readiness program (AVID).

In the process noted earlier, Michael got to select about half his teachers because they were in specialized areas. He felt he had the double advantage of being a well-known and -liked principal with a school in an attractive neighborhood, and the teachers he requested and the ones asked to transfer to his school accepted. One of his worries with that process was that if he ended up with a number of young teachers, he would invest in specific training for them and then "Boom!" (his word) they could be gone because of seniority layoffs.

Michael felt well supported by the district and his fellow PLC colleagues in the process of creating a new magnet school with a new image. The district helped him market the school to the neighborhood, and the PLC group proved to be a dependable resource for ideas and support. He also was particularly complimentary of the leaders who supported him in central office; he believes they are good at what they do because they were all principals at one time. Michael also noted that this experience helped him understand just how much influence a principal had on being able to attract teachers at a school, and he felt there was a similar appreciation from principals for their superintendent.

Other than the visual arts academy, one of the biggest differences between Michael's PLC school and his past school was that he had not reviewed data as much at his previous school because it was high-performing in almost every area. Now he reviews data constantly and is closely involved in adjusting instruction and working with teachers. He also received a lot of support to help his students and teachers succeed.

Like Denver, Long Beach implements school choice, so no formal feeder patterns exist; the PLC schools were some of the first to have the opportunity to work with other similar schools. However, to ensure that the choice policy did not run counter to Michael's goal of bringing back the neighborhood students, the superintendent told the families around the new Marshall Academy of the Arts that they had to attend that school. While there was pushback at first, the next year parents voiced their approval of the school. Thus, there were no students bused to Marshall that second year. Ironically, it also meant that the demographics at the school shifted to a wealthier student body, and the school lost its Title I status. However, since those funds had been centralized anyway, their loss did not affect Michael's school budget.

At the October open house in 2010, 10 percent of its parents visited Marshall; in 2011, the number was 70 percent. When asked about the impact of the new academy on student achievement, Michael said Marshall's API went up 49 points, making it the highest API among the PLC schools. Whether that increase is due to the instructional changes in the school, the shift of the student population, or both remains to be seen. However, Marshall is now a school with a strong academic program where parents want to send their children.

Mary Butler Visual & Performing Arts Magnet

Denise had loved her previous school, where she had spent nine years and brought it from an API of 500 to 751. Upon hearing that she was being requested to lead a different school, she "cried for two weeks." Then, she said, "I got over my shock of the change, and decided to focus on the students. I was needed by the students and community, and I knew I could transform the school." However, Denise said the real change started when she was in the classrooms, something that had not happened in that school for a number of years.

Denise is a veteran principal with an enthusiastic, no-nonsense, "tell-it-like-it-is" personality. She told teachers that she would take them out of their comfort zone, and she worked hard to observe them frequently, review data with them, and help them reflect on their instruction and how it could be improved. When, at the beginning of her second year, she asked staff members what they had heard about her, they told her they had heard that she could be tough and that she would be in their classrooms, but also that she would be fair. In fact, in the first few weeks of that year, her schedule became hectic and she wasn't able to get into classrooms. Teachers began seeking her out to ask why they hadn't visited them yet. Denise was elated: "I love that cultural shift with the staff. Now department meetings are really collaborative and focused on students."

The culture shift was also helped by the school's forty-nine-point API gain, which marks a big skip within California's accountability system. When some teachers found that increase to be "unbelievable," Denise challenged them, asking, "Why don't you believe it?" This led to them "tackling the elephant in the room," and studying a book by Ruby Payne, an expert in, "changing the mindsets of economic classes and crossing socioeconomic lines in education and work, as well as for social change."[3] Denise attributes the achievement gains to focusing on data—not giving teachers too many strategies to address at once—and focusing on fidelity of implementing the curriculum. In addition to not having used data before at the school, the teachers did not have much experience with understanding how to construct effective re-teaching lessons.

This year things are going smoothly, teachers are applying their new knowledge in the classroom, and Denise says she couldn't be happier. In our interview, she said, "As a matter of fact, just yesterday I told Chris [Steinhauser], 'You knew what was best for me when I did not know it. This was the best move for me.' He saw something in me that I didn't see." Denise believes professionals should always stretch themselves and be stretched. She recalled what Carl Cohen said to her years ago, when he was leading the district: "Denise, if you make everyone happy, you aren't doing your job." She now sees the move as an honor and is enthusiastically looking forward to the remainder of this year.

CONCLUSION

While some Long Beach schools are not performing as well as the district feels they should, none of its schools has fallen under "corrective action" for failure to meet AYP. Since this district was not involved with the SIG program, it provides a good example of a coherent system that has been a strong, consistent performer among urban districts for a number of years. The fact that the district has had two decades of strong leadership in the superintendent's office has helped provide it with stability, trust, and lack of the typical churn often found in urban districts. It will be interesting to see outcomes from the sixth-grade academy after a year or two of implementation.

8

COMPARING APPROACHES: EXTERNAL-PARTNER-LED, DISTRICT-LED, AND CHARTER PARTNERS

There seems to be two schools of thought about whether external partners are necessary for executing the difficult work of school turnaround. School turnaround is something that some districts have the capacity to do on their own—perhaps with some tools and guidance—but sometimes it requires external expertise to lead the process in partnership with districts. This chapter explores the thinking and circumstances that leads to these different paths and further considers the question, if turnaround does require external partners, then how do districts fund those partnerships, and do they ever get to a point where they can sustain the reform effort or strategies autonomously?

Whether external-partner- or district-led, turnarounds in some of the districts profiled included bringing in charter management organizations. The third section in this chapter examines the reasons for and effects of this aspect of turnaround.

EXTERNAL-PARTNER–LED TURNAROUND

Take a district that has a number of chronically failing schools and years of school reform that resulted primarily in low-yield outcomes that moved the needle sporadically at best in a handful of schools. Add to that the reality of high leader and teacher turnover and practice churn that is often found in districts that have a significant number of schools in "school improvement." It seems logical that an outside organization could lend expertise, fresh perspective, convening power, and perhaps political cover to improve what many see as past failed processes.

Mass Insight

Mass Insight Education, a national nonprofit focused on school improvement, is a well-known player in the turnaround field. The organization has authored several important reports and tools that have influenced current turnaround practices and policies.[1] The School Turnaround Group (STG) is a division of Mass Insight that partners with school districts and state education agencies to redesign the way districts support their lowest-performing schools. Mass Insight proposes that districts create an autonomous zone for their struggling schools, and that they engage with an external *lead partner* to help align the work of all the outside programs and partners.

I had the opportunity to speak to Justin Cohen, president of the STG, and Mike Contompasis, senior field consultant, about their work.[2] According to Cohen and Contompasis, to mitigate the effects of poverty, school systems need to create readiness to learn, readiness to teach, and readiness to act. They explain that one of the challenges principals face, is that in order to act, they often must break rules imposed by central office. The concern at STG is that few districts are doing turnaround work systemically, with the exception of the Chicago Office of School Turnaround, Charlotte-Mecklenburg with its Achievement Zone, and Mastery Public Charter. STG believes that some of the things holding districts back are lack of institutional memory resulting from high leader turnover and an insufficient pipeline of leaders who have the specific skills required to turn schools around. Another variable that is further from district control is the ability to "clear the bureaucratic underbrush" that impedes school turnaround—issues like inflexible teacher union bargaining agreements and state requirements around time, labor, and management.

To offset those obstacles, Cohen and Contompasis contend, districts need to build an internal cadre of people who can collaborate to "withstand any external nonsense that goes on" by establishing a cohort of schools that can be insulated from those rules and policies. To help districts mitigate the many levels involved with clearing the underbrush, STG offers a variety of services, including assisting clusters of schools to become flexible "mini-districts" through their Partnership Zone Initiative; assisting districts with building the local capacity of their schools; working through its State Development Network to implement new statewide policy frameworks for school turnaround; and working with state legislators to create policies that allow states and districts more flexibility to implement their choice of turnaround strategies.[3]

When a district works with STG-appointed lead partners, the governance of the turnaround effort is largely in control of the partner, as is outlined by STG's contract with the district. The three- to five-year contract agrees that the partner will lead a small "intentional" cluster of schools in which programs and systems will be aligned; assume authority for decision making on school staffing; provide core academic and student support services; and engage extensively (five days per week) with each school. According to STG, the lead partner model is a good proposition for those interested in turnaround work because program implementation can be consistently managed; the lead partners have control over people, time, and money; states and districts will agree to relinquish rights to impose interventions on the lead partners during their contract time; lead partners can leverage existing facilities and other district infrastructure like transportation; and they can choose to outsource certain operational services. According to STG, Mastery Charter, one of Philadelphia's charter school partners, is one of the few organizations that functions with a similar lead partner model.

Sacramento City Unified School District

The only districts presented in this book that engaged with an external partner, outside of vendors that assisted with specialized portions of the work, were SCUSD and the Denver Public Schools. The turnaround work in Sacramento was implemented by a new incoming superintendent in conjunction with the development of a new strategic plan and central office reorganization. Superintendent Jonathan Raymond was familiar with Rochelle Herring-Peniston and her company, Transformation by Design, and knew that she could lead SCUSD's Data Inquiry work strategically and "brilliantly." Herring-Peniston had previously done similar work in Massachusetts and came prepared with tools and a plan. However, upon arrival, she found that the schools had been told they could design their own programs, so she had to navigate having them correctly implement components of Data Inquiry without taking their design autonomy away. She also had to change her original plan for her SCUSD work when she found the need for an additional component that would address improving instructional practices. She was very intent on building internal turnaround capacity; to this end, she worked hard to teach the components of data inquiry and instructional improvement within the framework of having school personnel develop the inquiry process on their own, and then reflect on it.

The organic process characterized by Data Inquiry was difficult at first, explained Herring-Peniston, because the principals were accustomed to being leaders who had answers, which runs counter to the nature of the inquiry process. In her words, "People have to be comfortable leading with questions and being asked to put student and professional work on the table; it's a different approach than they've seen in the past. It's hard—there's no roadmap." Because she worked for short, intense periods in the district and then went back to her home out of state, school personnel frequently expressed that they needed more time with her. She described he situation as balancing the process of helping them become comfortable with a different type of process and understanding the stress they were experiencing through their urgency and desire to improve student achievement. However, district personnel's reflections, recorded in data inquiry logs, changed from voicing frustration to displaying enthusiasm and progress with the process toward the end of the initial year.

Herring-Peniston's other challenge as an external partner was trying to help school leaders and teachers see the data inquiry and instructional work as an embedded part of their overall strategy and daily activities, rather than just "add-on professional development." To embed it into the district's overall strategy, she strove to align her work with the district and other personnel in the Priority Schools by meeting with the superintendent and other cabinet leaders on a regular basis, often at the same time to keep everyone on the same page.

When asked how she was working with the district to help it achieve autonomy, she explained that her approach is to develop a cross-functional team of district and school leaders who learn how to implement the strategies. The challenge with building a strong foundation in Sacramento to sustain the work is that staff members get trained and then disappear due to layoffs at the schools and central office. If a district cannot build organizational capacity, according to Herring-Peniston, then an outside partner might be required. Were the right conditions in place, however, a cross-functional team of teachers, principals, and district-level staff would begin the transition from being those "who learn the work" by shadowing the partner to serving as an apprentice who does some of the work.

Herring-Peniston has been working with districts on school improvement and turnaround for almost twelve years, and she shared some advice with me on how to best leverage external partnerships:

- Have a logic model in place. Whether it is created together or brought in, certain things needs to be laid out explicitly.
- Engage in joint planning, ideally by using the data inquiry cycle. Then you can create it together, execute it, and reflect on it as a regularly scheduled activity.
- Commit to and calendar time to debrief.

Denver Public Schools

DPS is the other district that engaged the assistance of an external partner, not to the same extent as Sacramento, but as oversight more than as a skill-specific partner organization or consultant. Denver began its turnaround work the first year by planning and putting initial structures in place. It's likely that, at that point, district leaders knew what they wanted to do, but they still needed to assess their capacity to identify if they needed any assistance. Once the district decided to take on a larger and more complex regional approach, it engaged the assistance of the Blueprint Schools Network (Blueprint), an organization with a strong reputation that focused on elements that aligned well with the Denver Plan. While there was not enough time to interview Blueprint's leader, who assisted with the Far Northeast regional strategy, the district leader who oversaw that work said that Blueprint was an invaluable thought partner and provided an important, focused resource for oversight, objective data, and assistance with executing the work with all the schools.

DPS also worked extensively with charter schools, a relationship that will be discussed later in this chapter.

DISTRICT-LED TURNAROUND

Charlotte-Mecklenburg Schools, the School District of Philadelphia, and the Long Beach Unified School District chose to implement their turnaround strategy from within their own system. While all three districts organized their turnaround schools in one area similar to STG's partnership zone model, they each also built their strategy as an initiative that would impact and improve practices across the entire district. An analysis of the similarities and differences between the strategies and context of these three districts provides interesting information to help districts decide which approach might work best for them.

Charlotte-Mecklenburg Schools

CMS is a district that gained (or regained, depending on how you view its history) stability and a positive image when Peter Gorman came on board as superintendent in 2006. Compared with other districts, CMS had the advantage of having a veteran leader who was implementing a far-reaching, labor-intensive approach in a nonunionized state. Though we cannot easily determine whether these variables contributed to the gains CMS made, the lack of restrictions often imposed by teacher unions around the use of time and people may have cleared away some potential impediments.

Charlotte-Mecklenburg did engage the assistance of numerous organizations for targeted activities; for instance, New Leaders for New Schools was brought in to help with teacher hiring and the Aspiring Leaders program for leadership training. While these external organizations provided targeted assistance in specific areas, the district appeared to have the capacity to build and implement their strategy and engage expertise as needed.

Long Beach Unified School District

Long Beach also chose to lead its own turnaround work, partly because it was clear that these efforts would be better received if implemented from within the system. Additionally, as superintendent Chris Steinhauser pointed out, Long Beach is a district that has the capacity to implement the work. Of all the districts presented in this book, Long Beach has the most leadership stability, and it is a well-aligned, high-functioning organization. Given those conditions, an external partner might not as easily be able to navigate the entrenched culture of "the Long Beach Way," which according to interviewees, proved to be very successful.

WORKING WITH CHARTERS

Two of the schools in this study also worked extensively with charter management organizations: Philadelphia, with a district-led turnaround effort, and Denver, which had partnered with an external expert. While both efforts provided something different and often innovative for students, charters were much easier to establish in a charter-friendly city like Denver than Philadelphia, where there was active resistance to the introduction of charters.

School District of Philadelphia

In Philadelphia, as with CMS, district leader Arlene Ackerman felt that she did not need the assistance of an external partner because she saw herself as an "experienced turnaround specialist." However, the district did partner with several charter management organizations (CMOs), including Mastery, which STG had cited as an organization that functioned very like their lead partner model. When I asked Ackerman about her partnership with CMOs, she said that she was leery of them at first. She was concerned that they would cherry-pick their students rather than serve all students in the charter's neighborhood. However, her concern was not borne out; she found the charters to provide a good viable option for some of Philadelphia's struggling schools. In her words: "If they [charters] take all of the children in neighborhood and turn those schools around, I think in the long run it's fair to have open market. When it comes to reforming schools, the criteria, evaluation, and monitoring all have to be the same. As long as it's fair [to students] and they [charters] are held to same standard, I don't care what organization it happens to be."

Ackerman's reference to monitoring was in regard to the pushback she received from some district schools at her decision to compare them to the CMO Renaissance schools. Before many CMOs came on, the district provided comparison charts of schools to demographically matched "peer" schools, and then to all of the schools in the district. Ackerman's reasoning was that she did not want schools to aim for being the best of a struggling group of schools; rather, she wanted them to aim to be the best out of all of the schools. Once the CMOs became partners, she decided to include them in those comparisons, to provide information to the schools and to parents to help them be "informed consumers about their schools."

As described in chapter 4, CMOs in Philadelphia are selected through an RFQ process to be vetted for their capacity, track record with student achievement, fiscal stability, curriculum approach, and turnaround plan. Once recommended to the superintendent, they go into a pool, where they can go through a matching process to be voted on by the school committee, 51 percent of whom are parents and the rest school leaders and teachers. For the matching process, the CMOs provide the school committee with a written evaluation, make an oral presentation, host site visits, and meet with community members. In 2010, there were twenty CMO applications to Philadelphia; out of those, ten were selected to complete the RFP process and six were selected for the matching process (since only six Renaissance school models were approved by the board that year).

The entire CMO selection and matching process is overseen by a specific department, staffed by one person in the district, who also monitors them to ensure students are doing appropriately well. Thus, the charter director ensures that the CMOs are closely scrutinized, well matched, and selected by the community around the proposed school. When Arlene Ackerman asked parents what fueled their choice to send their children to a charter school, the primary reason was safety. Other district personnel hypothesized that it was because charters represented something different from a past failing school, and that charters do a good job of marketing their strengths.

The main areas that charters had autonomy over in Philadelphia were time and personnel. If a charter sees fit to start school a week early to orient and train teachers or extend school hours, it can do so easily. In Philadelphia, teachers who choose to work in charters are no longer members of the teachers' union, although they are essentially pressing "pause" on their union status and can rejoin when they choose. When I asked how teacher salaries compare between charter and noncharter schools, I was told that for teachers with five years of experience and under, the pay was similar, but for senior teachers it was higher in the district. Teachers mainly chose to teach in Philadelphia's charter schools because of location or because they had taught at the school when it was part of the district.

Rahim Islam, chief executive officer of Universal Companies, one of the district's other providers, described the charter climate in Philadelphia as "mixed." Because Philadelphia is a union town, there is a "mixed bag" of understanding about charters and what exactly they are. Islam felt that politics had a big influence on the acceptance of charters in states and districts, and that Republicans tended to support charter schools, while Democrats largely did not. Islam opined that charters would be an accepted model whenever the political power was behind them, and when it was not, "they will be completely left out of the equation." However, he believes that the success of charters has been proven to a certain degree, and overall, it would be "hard to get the genie back in the bottle at this point."

Denver Public Schools

Charters in Denver appear to be working well, likely because the state is seen as being very "charter-friendly" and has a history of tolerance for innovation. In fact, DPS has its own Office of School Reform and Innovation that oversees the DPS District-Charter Collaboration Compact, which establishes equity in accountability measures (the district is also evaluated on the School Performance Framework), outlines joint commitments between charters and district-run schools, and then outlines separate commitments for each entity. The compact is laid out in three phases: from November 2010 to March 2012; March 2012 to November 2012; and November 2012 to November 2013.[4] In addition to managing the compact, the Office of School Reform and Innovation works closely with the school turnaround leaders. A number of schools in Denver shared facilities with charters. Building sharing is an arrangement that works well for charters; in many states, for example, Texas, one of the biggest hurdles charters face is finding and funding their facilities.[5] In states where charters must have an established facility as part of the application process, funding a building becomes somewhat of a chicken and egg dilemma. With the ability to share a building as they do in Denver, charters are provided with a facility, food service, and transportation.

DPS superintendent Tom Boasberg also agreed that Denver has a strong relationship with CMOs, and that the district welcomes the opportunity to work with high-performing charter schools. Reflecting the tenets outlined in the compact, he asserted that the focus is for the schools to meet the unique needs of students, regardless of where the oversight rests; thus, they share a lot of resources as well as accountability structures.

Advantages and Disadvantages of Charters

The advantage of charters cited by Denver and Philadelphia was that they provided a viable option to serve students and improve schools that had failed in the past. They also have flexibility with time, money, and personnel, and thus are able to create some programs and implement interventions that some district schools cannot. The ability to bring back students into their neighborhoods and for the district schools to learn from the charters was also seen as a huge plus. For charters, the biggest advantage was the ability to access a facility and share other resources like transportation and access to sports. For practitioners and reformers, strong partnerships between charters and districts are helpful for scaling promising practices that would not otherwise happen with one-school boutique models.

The disadvantages cited by interviewees are that charters require positive political will to seen as a viable option. They also potentially can pose competition for funds via student enrollment and for teachers. Although the districts partnering with charters did not voice concern about them, these disadvantages are seen as a big obstacle in some areas; some districts that feel that teachers or students are being poached by charters. In

Philadelphia, the teachers' union lost membership whenever a teacher took a position with a charter; thus, the union strongly opposed the creation of more charter-led schools. Additionally, the process of selecting charters in Philadelphia became embroiled in political corruption, resulting in the resignation of two lead board members.

Even in nonunion states, districts sometimes see charters as competition. In Houston, when a neighboring charter system, Knowledge is Power Program, expanded in 2010, headlines in the *Houston Chronicle* read, "Houston ISD Loses Four More Principals to KIPP."[6] In the article, the superintendent has a quote about "welcoming the competition." Perhaps it is for some of those reasons that Sacramento, Long Beach, and Charlotte-Mecklenburg choose not to utilize charters as a component of their turnaround efforts.

The one concern in using charters as a turnaround partner is the potential for districts to not closely engage with them to ensure that students in their community are getting a good education, and to miss opportunities to leverage their external social capital or strategies. While Philadelphia made some efforts to collaborate informally with its charter partners, it did include them in their accountability comparisons. Denver's District-Charter Collaboration Compact provides a great model for how to formalize the process to gain the most from what could be a mutually beneficial partnership.

DISCUSSION

The question of whether to engage with what STG refers to as *lead partners* depends on the capacity of each organization, as well as the culture and relationships. Philadelphia,

Charlotte-Mecklenburg, and Long Beach chose not to engage external lead partners. These districts had experienced leaders and plans they wanted to implement, and they had the capacity and infrastructure to do it. Long Beach had the strongest infrastructure, since it was implementing its strategy within an already high-functioning organization. In contrast, while they initially did not completely have the infrastructure or talent, Charlotte-Mecklenburg and Philadelphia received additional funding through the School Improvement Grant (SIG) to build them.

Denver began its turnaround work on its own, created its strategy and infrastructure partly through the SIG, and then engaged some external assistance in the second year, once it had identified its needs. Sacramento had a new superintendent who had to completely rebuild the district's infrastructure and had little funds to implement any plan on a large scale. Thus, the district engaged with an external consultant who worked jointly with district personnel to implement the strategy.

Culture also influenced the decision to work with partners or not. The willingness and acceptance to work with external partners, the perceived uniqueness of the school culture, and size and scope of the turnaround effort all factor into such a decision. Long Beach's superintendent Chris Steinhauser believed that his staff would not respond as well to a strategy implemented by an external organization or consultant. Sacramento's superintendent chose to have his external consultant work in conjunction with his staff. However, in Philadelphia, partners were seen as a tool to link with the community, but worked rather separately from district staff. Charter schools provided an ability to help "repackage" schools for neighborhoods that could not get past the bad reputation of the original chronically failing school. In some cases, an external partner might be helpful for being able to convene stakeholders with different opinions about turnaround strategies, or provide political cover so that districts can attribute certain decisions to the organization or gain certain autonomies through the partnership, as described by STG with lead partners, or by charters with their flexibility in managing time and personnel.

CONCLUSION

In sum, there appears to be no definitive answer to whether districts or schools should engage with external partners to implement their turnaround plan. The decision depends on the district's capacity to manage and implement the reform, the skill level of the staff, the size of the approach, and the availability of funds to pay for partners. Although the district not receiving SIG funds did not cite funding as a barrier to soliciting external partnerships, it could possibly be an issue in other districts. Other factors important to weigh in the decision to engage with external partners are the culture's responsiveness to "outsiders" and the existing political structures that could either push back on or function better with potential partners.

9

❧

LEARNING FROM TURNAROUNDS

The purpose of this book is to drive the dialogue and vision of school turnaround beyond a prescriptive school-
by-school approach to scaling it at the district level. Scaling
turnaround is important because past school-led approaches
have either failed to move beyond incremental gains or were
unsustainable. Several studies attribute these poor results to
schools' lack of capacity to implement far-reaching or innovative changes, primarily because of limited ability to align and
manage resources often controlled by districts, like personnel,
funds, and in some cases curriculum and instruction.[1] Additionally, school-led reform efforts do not utilize the power of
districts to coordinate and align supports, skills, and knowledge and mitigate political and cultural obstacles to make a
substantive change to the instructional core.

While I've always felt that high-functioning, aligned systems
(rather than individual schools) serve more students well, the
fiscal constraints that districts and states have been experiencing since around 2010 add an important dimension to the

ongoing debate about whether to centralize or decentralize educational decision making and resources. Aside from the issue of educational equity, efficiency is now of prime concern. With the unprecedented amount of funds being dedicated to improving the bottom-performing 5 percent of our nation's schools, we must ensure that those soon-to-be fleeting funds are well invested to sustain what is achieved through programs like SIG and Race to the Top.

One of my all-time favorite quotes is Tom Payzant's explanation of why he became the superintendent of Boston Public Schools: "I wanted to take a medium-size district and create a school system, rather than a system of schools." Payzant would often emphasize the importance of using a systems approach to school reform, rather than "letting a thousand flowers bloom on their own." Now it seems we must consider an additional question: Is it *fiscally* efficient and effective to let a thousand flowers bloom on their own?

The evidence leads to a resounding no for a plethora of reasons, the first being that children's education should not hinge on their zip code. Second, students in urban districts move around, making instructional alignment across schools important so that students do not experience fragmentation in their educational programs. Alignment also helps create a seamless program within school feeder patterns, which is important for ensuring that students are well prepared for each transition level throughout school. After all, it would be fruitless to improve instruction in an elementary school, only to have those instructional gains be lost if those students flow to a poor-performing middle school.

From the organizational perspective, alignment is best driven from a centralized source that is focused on providing oversight, lending expertise, and providing support and re-sources. As I noted in chapter 2, the district is well positioned to serve as that resource for clarifying what is to be taught and learned; helping schools obtain effective talent; providing con-tinuous data and monitoring systems; assisting with the devel-opment of student, staff, and school interventions; and help-ing garner appropriate political will and manage relationships.

The Norfolk (Virginia) Public Schools district provides a good example. Before John Simpson became superintendent, the district decentralized instructional program selection, with the result that its elementary schools were implementing at least twenty-five different reading programs. Thus, a first-grade student in school A who moved across town to school B might find herself repeating previous instruction, skipping key ele-ments that that had not been covered in school A, or struggling to learn a completely different reading approach. If that stu-dent moved multiple times, which is not uncommon in urban districts, the potential variability multiplied with every move. When Simpson arrived in Norfolk, he recentralized program se-lection and, through a committee, selected one research-based reading program that ended up raising reading scores across the district. In addition to improving achievement, the selec-tion of the single reading program cut costs by making staff training, books, professional development, and evaluation of the program easier to coordinate and to repurpose as needed.

When Arne Duncan became U.S. Secretary of Education in 2009, he was aware of the challenges facing large urban districts. As chief executive officer of the Chicago Public Schools from 2001–2008, he had done work similar to that described in the five districts featured in this book, in a district that had many similar challenges. When Duncan announced the $3.5 billion

SIG grant, he referenced some of those challenges: "If we are to put an end to stubborn cycles of poverty and social failure, and put our country on track for long-term economic prosperity, we must address the needs of children who have long been ignored and marginalized in chronically low-achieving schools."[2]

The SIG channeled a massive influx of funds into states and districts to support them in making a significant change for chronically failing schools. It provided guidance on how states could select districts and begin to plan the work, and it set forth requirements that represented strategies that most educators agree are crucial for bringing about the change needed in poor-performing schools. The districts highlighted in this book are engaged in this extremely difficult work, using a districtwide approach. While there is a high level of interest and funding behind turnaround, it is still a relatively new field (at least in this specific iteration) with only preliminary data on short-term implementation and virtually no information on how it can be scaled at the district level. The districts in this book did not all apply for or receive a SIG grant, but they all included many of the practices suggested in SIG's planning and designing guidance, as well as the required strategies outlined in the grant's transformation model.

The remainder of this chapter compares the different turnaround strategies being implemented in each district, taking care to consider how the districts developed and implemented their models and strategies and what levers and barriers helped or hindered them along the way. Given that each district saw performance increases in at least some of their target schools, a comparison of how they addressed the required strategies in SIG could potentially be useful for understanding how the policy has worked in application. The chapter concludes with lessons for practitioners who are interested in district-led turnaround.

ORGANIZATIONAL STRUCTURES AND OVERSIGHT

Whether they were applying for the SIG grant or not, the five districts featured in this book sought to build a strategy around their most struggling schools and identify those schools by selecting a certain number of their lowest performers on the basis of student achievement. Also in common was their decision to embed that strategy in the overall district strategic plan rather than treat it as an "add-on" program. Connecting their turnaround approach to the overall district plan created the ability to oversee it from the superintendent's office and to arrange the schools in some type of cohort to enable more focused oversight and support for the schools by a dedicated central office leader.

Charlotte-Mecklenburg Schools

Charlotte-Mecklenburg put its selected eleven schools in what it calls the Achievement Zone, representing six geographic areas that function as professional learning communities (PLCs). The AZ schools are provided the "best" leaders for certain areas in central office, are always first in line for services, and are overseen by an area superintendent whose sole focus is to support them. After the first year of implementation, CMS created a districtwide human capital strategy that is the backdrop of its turnaround work. Because it had the capacity and appropriate conditions to implement the turnaround plan on its own, CMS chose to not engage an external partner to lead the work. However, it does seek help from several organizations for specific strategies.

Sacramento City Unified School District and Long Beach Unified School District

The Sacramento and Long Beach models have a number of similarities, including the same state (California) and comparable numbers of schools and students. Neither received SIG funds, and California is one of the states hardest hit by education budget cuts. However, both districts still decided to identify a small number of schools to focus on for improvement, and to parse those schools out into cohorts that would function as PLCs. Both districts also have leaders who believe in systemic reform approaches and thus view their small cohorts as places to pilot strategies to potentially scale across their districts.

The districts' approaches differ somewhat in oversight and implementation, although both are driven from the superintendent's office and have strategies that are part of their districts' strategic plan. Sacramento's six Priority Schools report directly to the chief accountability officer, who provides them her full attention, additional resources, and "protection" from central office policies or requests that would distract them from their work. To assist with formulating the work and develop and implement the training for its approach, the district also engaged the assistance of an external turnaround partner.

While Sacramento's Priority Schools are in both elementary and secondary schools, the eight schools identified by Long Beach are all middle schools. As in Sacramento, the eight Long Beach schools function like (and are called) PLC schools. However, the Long Beach schools are overseen informally by the superintendent and formally by a director with a research background who can help test and share new tools across the

PLC schools and district. To help connect and support the group, the district has engaged as coaches three retired principals who had strong track records in turning around middle schools in the district.

An additional difference in the structure of Long Beach's model is its decision to segment out all of the sixth-graders from the eight PLCs into self-contained sixth-grade academy. The rationale was to mitigate problems the district found when students transitioned from the fifth to the sixth grade. Putting the sixth-graders in their own building gave their principal and teachers complete flexibility over the schedule and student interventions during the entire school day. The final difference between the two California districts is that Long Beach, having a well-established, high-functioning system, did not engage the assistance of an external partner.

Denver Public Schools

Denver's turnaround approach is more complex in that it involves multiple funding structures that represent a combination of federal and philanthropic dollars. The DPS model also provides a wide array of school configurations (K–6, K–8, district-led, charter-led, for example), some of which are transitioning into different grade levels, splitting into two schools, or sharing buildings between two schools. While the variety and changes are bold and innovative, they also make counting the schools extremely difficult. What connects and organizes DPS's strategy is the fact that many of its low-performing schools are located within two distinct areas, prompting the district to organize its turnaround efforts into two regions: the West Denver Turnaround Schools and the Far Northeast Turnaround Schools.

209

The West Denver turnaround schools are overseen by the West Denver Network Schools. They consist of three elementary schools, two middle schools, a K–8 school, a K–9 school being phased into a K–12, two high schools, and third high school that is being phased into two 6–12 academies. Models outside of traditional schools included in West Denver are a Montessori school, an International Baccalaureate school, and an arts school. The West Denver Network is overseen by an executive and a deputy director from the district office, who are supported by a district school improvement partner and a parent involvement coordinator.

The Far Northeast turnaround schools are led by the Denver Summit Schools Network (DSSN). While the network represents two different communities, both are located in an isolated region of the city. Likely some of these schools are also in transition; however, DSSN currently lists ten: a collegiate prep academy, two international schools, three elementary schools, a middle school, a high school, a high-tech early college high school, and a community arts school. The DSSN is overseen by a central office executive director, who closely works with Blueprint Schools Network, which developed the school reform strategy that the region follows and assists with monitoring implementation and outcomes.

In addition to focusing its cohorts in feeder patterns and regions, Denver is also partnering with CMOs to share buildings with several of their schools. For the district, the CMO partnerships have helped recover a number of students who left their neighborhood school or district. The partnership has also helped fill partially vacant buildings and led to valuable cross-collaboration among different school models. For charters, the model has been helpful for providing facilities and other important services like transportation and school food services. As an additional indirect outcome, the arrangement has helped blur the boundaries between charter- and district-led schools in the district, and by putting the charters under the same accountability system, it has helped identify a number of underperforming CMOs.

Denver has used its multiple funding sources to create a dedicated Office of School Turnaround that coordinates the two regional efforts. Staffed by a reform-minded director, the turnaround office also has a dedicated finance and operations manager. The director and finance manager often meet together as a team, along with the two West and Far Northeast regional directors. The entire team has worked to help codify the district's turnaround work so that it can be easily understood by various stakeholders, and various documents clearly outline the district's process for selecting and supporting its turnaround schools. Having a turnaround office to lead its turnaround strategy has been especially helpful for aligning DPS's ambitious and innovative approach, as well as the oversight and support provided to the schools.

School District of Philadelphia

Being a significantly larger district (at least in the number of schools) than the other four profiled in this book, Philadelphia has the most far-reaching turnaround approach, with 95 of its 257 schools being targeted for the effort. Philadelphia initiated its turnaround approach in 2008 and also arranged the targeted schools in a cohort and called them Empowerment schools. The Empowerment schools received individually targeted supports, a parent ombudsman, additional volunteers, and assistance from Empowerment School Response (ESR) teams—fifteen teams of trained educators working with staff in ten regions and the central office. Oversight for all of the Empowerment schools was provided by the regional superintendents.

What first began in 2008 as Empowerment schools evolved in 2010 with the addition of two more tiers to the model and a new name: Renaissance schools. There were seven Year 1 Renaissance schools and five Year 2 schools. While moving that many schools out from being managed by the district, Philadelphia added a charter school division to central office, where one director managed the process of vetting CMOs, matching them to schools, and monitoring their progress. Other than relatively new attempts on the part of the CMOs and somewhat by the district, the CMOs and districts are beginning to collaborate, although infrequently and on an informal basis. Clear lines seem to separate the Promise Academies and Renaissance schools, as the Renaissance schools are barely visible and deeply embedded in the district's website. Though Denver also worked with CMOs, they treated them more as part of the district by co-sharing buildings and listing them on their website alongside district-led schools.

Districts must make many decisions when embarking on a strategy designed to dramatically improve instruction in chronically failing schools. One of the first considerations is how to structurally organize, place, and govern the work. While each district I profiled had some very different approaches to how their models were implemented in schools, there were many commonalities regarding where the program was placed, how it was imbedded as an overall district strategy, and how schools were organized.

Where a program is driven from is extremely important, particularly if it is intended to be integrated into the district's overall strategy and connect to elements of work in multiple central office divisions. All five districts in this book placed their strategies within the superintendent's division. Turnaround work requires thinking systemically about how curriculum and instruction, professional development, human resources, performance management tools, accountability, communications, and relationship management can come together to improve instruction. Placing oversight at the highest administrative level—the superintendent's office—allows leaders of the work to tap into all the above departments and connect the work to the overall strategic plan, and it provides a signal to the district and community that turnaround (or school improvement) is a district priority.

In addition to similar program placement, the districts all organized their struggling schools into a cohort structure, which in of itself brings scale and alignment to their strategies. The main advantage of using a cohort model is the ability to create a community of support and learning for personnel who are leading difficult work that often is new to them. A cohort can also provide alignment across schools that are often in similar regions or feeder patterns, and it makes coordination of oversight, training, and performance management easier to implement and manage.

Decisions about whether to engage an external partner and how to arrange oversight depend on the capacity of the district's central office to lead difficult and demanding change. It also depends on the availability of funding and political support as well as the ability of the system to tolerate innovation and deviations from policy and entrenched customs and practices. The internal capacity assessment and the size and needs of a district's schools can also inform the important decision about how far-reaching a turnaround strategy should be. While some districts, like Sacramento and Long Beach, were limited by funds, they had some distinct advantages of implementing their turnaround on a smaller scale—mainly that they were able to more easily isolate program effects to inform which practices they wanted to export across the district.

HUMAN CAPITAL STRATEGIES

Turning around chronically failing schools requires making dramatic changes in schools and districts. This extremely difficult work cannot be done without district leaders who can identify school needs and create innovative solutions; school leaders who can break through long-embedded cultures of failure and change the focus and energy to students; teachers who can trust in trying something new and commit to helping their students reach high standards; and an integrated system that systemically supports all levels of personnel to help them successfully meet their goals.

All five districts incorporated human capital strategies into their turnaround efforts and placed a premium on having the right talent in place to implement their plans. While all agreed that turnaround requires a specific type of leader and strong teachers, labor union contracts limited some districts' choice of strategies. How each district leveraged flexibility and innovation and worked through obstacles provides interesting lessons for districts that function in various contexts.

Leadership

All five case study districts chose to implement their turn-around work by replacing current principals (unless they were at their schools two years or less) with principals they perceived as being stronger and/or having a proven track record with improving student achievement. Most principals saw it as an honor to be asked to move to a turnaround school, and Charlotte-Mecklenburg specifically marketed being identified as a principal for its Achievement Zone schools as being a high honor. Discussions with several district leaders revealed that they agreed that turning around schools required a different skill set than "maintaining" a school. One Philadelphia leader called turnaround principals "Green Beret" leaders who had the skills to make drastic changes and identify strong assistant principals and teachers. Philadelphia in particular seemed to be very purposeful about placing its leadership talent. It uses its Green Beret principals in its toughest schools to set a new culture and new practices. After a year or so, when the school becomes stable, the district will consider moving that leader to a different school and replacing him or her with a leader who has the skill to maintain the changes the Green Beret leader put in place.

To move its strongest principals into Achievement Zone schools, Charlotte-Mecklenburg motivated principals with a 10 percent raise, freedom from certain district rules, and the ability to choose an eight-person team, who would also receive raises. In addition to attracting the right talent, this strategy provided flexible conditions for the leaders to be innovative in their approaches, while supporting them in their move with an entire team.

The districts all had a program or plan to provide leadership training options for aspiring principals, new principals, and current principals. While four of the districts appeared to have a traditional approach to bringing in principal applicants, CMS allowed only leaders in the top bands of their forced ranking system into its top-level executive leadership program targeted for central office leaders.

In addition to ranking and targeting potential leaders, CMS's succession plan also included the identification and development of central office leaders. This practice seemed to be particularly valuable for ensuring that districts have a stable pipeline of key central office division leaders to support and sustain turnaround work over time.

Teachers

The ability of principals to select their own teachers made a big impact on their ability to dramatically improve instruction. Charlotte-Mecklenburg was the only district that did not have a formal teachers' union and thus had the most flexibility over what practices it could create around teachers. To that end, the district has been able to be more creative with teacher incentive and reward programs, including linking pay to student achievement growth. Despite this flexibility, CMS still found itself hundreds of teachers short before the beginning of the 2011–12 school year. To solve the problem, it engaged with the nationally based New Teacher Project to help with a large-scale recruiting and hiring effort.

The ability of the remaining four districts to implement policies and practices that affected teachers depended on the strength of the local teachers' union and the superintendents' ability to negotiate with the unions on the teacher contract. While Denver does have an organized teachers union, the district has been able to implement an innovative compensation structure, known as the ProComp program. Denver has also been able to incorporate student achievement measures in the new teacher evaluation system they are developing.

In Philadelphia, a city perceived by many as being a "strong union town," the district had almost no tools to incentivize teachers—who were extremely reluctant—to work in Promise Academies. While the district was able to hire and train a good number of new teachers, it lost many of them due to seniority-driven layoffs. The unions also impacted the district's ability to partner with charter schools, since charter teachers cannot be union members. Additionally, the union contract prevented the district from extending school hours or the school year or bringing in teachers outside of contract days or hours for professional development. In contrast, Denver was able to mitigate some of the same issues because charter teachers can still remain union members.

Principals in Long Beach and Sacramento get to select teachers only in certain specialty areas, such as bilingual education or literacy. Interestingly, leaders in Long Beach do not seem to complain about teacher quality, which may be attributed to the district's ability to attract teachers by virtue of its positive reputation, or because its close relationship with higher education institutions might be yielding an ample supply of effective teachers. Losing teachers trained specifically for Priority Schools was a concern in Sacramento; however, the union worked out an agreement with the district that teachers in Priority Schools will be left out of seniority layoffs if the district can provide documentation that those teachers received unique training for those specific schools.

Strategically managing human capital was a major focus for all five districts' turnaround efforts. Each district stressed the importance of having principals with a particular talent for managing change, building relationships, setting positive culture, and improving instruction. The district leaders who had any authority to at least select certain types of teachers often mentioned the difference effective teachers make on student achievement. One principal even stated that he could "guarantee" his results if he had to ability to select his entire teacher corps. However, districts that had to operate under a union contract faced far more challenges in recruiting, placing, and retaining the teachers they needed for their turnaround schools. In several cases, seniority rules cleared out entire departments in some schools that were overdependent on teachers new to the district. One district was able to offset that practice by working with the union to protect teachers in turnaround schools who had received very specified and different training from regular teachers. Additionally, union contracts kept several of the districts from using student growth measurements that tied student achievement scores to teachers.

CURRICULUM AND INSTRUCTION

Harvard professor Richard Elmore has written several pieces citing the tension he sees between "performance-based accountability demands" and improving "the instructional core." In systems that focus solely on test scores to improve student achievement it is probably true that there is a tension. However, interviews in all five districts represented in this book discussed how they were changing instruction—not focusing on test-taking skills—to improve student achievement.

Instruction in Long Beach has always been a top priority. District leaders have established a common academic language and provide pacing guides that clearly define what is to be taught and learned. The curriculum standards are implemented consistently through its Essential Elements of Effective Instruction, which outlines a set of instructional principles teachers are to follow, including using data to inform instruction and collaborating with others to align and improve teaching across grades. The district's history of a well-aligned and defined curriculum and instructional approach is likely a big contributor to its schools remaining off the state's "corrective action" list.

Like Long Beach, Sacramento uses data to drive the instructional process, providing another example of how outcomes can still drive high-quality instruction. While Sacramento thought its approach was going to focus primarily on better understanding student performance, its use of the Data Inquiry process led to a very in-depth collaborative process of looking at student work, discussing what high quality means for each student product, and analyzing and reflecting on how to better define expected outcomes by refining how tasks are written and presented. Though many reforms have a method for improving instruction, Sacramento's seemed to be a particularly creative way to do it with such a high level of scrutiny largely using the same set of teachers. Were the teachers to go to a staff development training and be told how to change instruction and then implement it on their own, they likely would have struggled. However, since their instructional analyses were done collaboratively and frequently, they were able to lean on each other for assistance.

In Charlotte-Mecklenburg, the focus was primarily on making sure the teachers understood the standards, were implementing them correctly, and knew how to create engaging lessons and re-teach as needed. The turnaround principals I interviewed in CMS both described how they personally work with teachers to improve instruction. The teachers involved in the Measuring Effective Teachers pilot funded by the Bill and Melinda Gates Foundation had the additional advantage of being able to observe and reflect on videos of themselves. One veteran teacher said that the project had really helped her target skills she felt she needed to improve upon.

Denver, like Long Beach, had a lot of traditional but effective curriculum and instruction strategies in place. It had backward-mapped the curriculum from college-to-career readiness down to kindergarten and had set performance targets for students, particularly at critical transition junctions like fifth and ninth grades. The district also worked on targeting interventions for students based on the frequent use of data and worked with principals on how to support teachers in literacy and mathematics.

Curriculum and instruction were both important elements in each of the districts' turnaround approaches. Some were more creative or intentional about specific instructional strategies to apply, and others focused more on implementing the curriculum with fidelity and matching interventions to students on an individual basis based on data. While the SIG requirements for transformation focus more on using data to drive instruction, they do not suggest that districts work to differentiate instruction for students or extend the curriculum beyond the state standards. However, all five districts used data to better refine instruction in a meaningful way that improved the instructional core, resulting in improved student achievement scores and student engagement.

PERFORMANCE MANAGEMENT

The use of data for performance management is not directly referenced in the basic high-level documents that outline the SIG requirements. However, how districts use data and other means to monitor student, teacher, and school performance on a continuous basis is crucial for providing immediate supports and interventions. Each district had its own set of tools to ensure that its efforts were helping it reach benchmarks and targets. CMS was very data-driven, as the superintendent often used data to gauge improvement across the district and in individual schools. One of the most interesting tools it used to assess leader and teacher effectiveness was a forced ranking tool driven by a detailed rubric designed to rank employee effectiveness from top to bottom. While some systems might use value-add data to gain more sensitivity to performance nuances, this tool sent a concrete signal about how performance aligned with job skills and was used to identify personnel for promotions as well as for layoffs, or, in their words, "shedding."

CMS also had a range of reports that guided much of the work and captured multiple student achievement data points as well as qualitative data about schools. The school progress reports, along with the externally led school quality reviews, provided information identifying schools' strengths and weaknesses and were used to guide the amount of flexibility granted to principals. CMS also used Data Wise, but not necessarily tied to instruction the same way it was applied in Sacramento. Sacramento used many similar performance-monitoring pieces, which is no surprise, since the superintendent used to be the chief accountability officer in CMS. Similar to Charlotte-Mecklenburg, Denver is also very data driven, and much of its work is informed by its School Performance Framework, which is designed to measure organizational strength and school performance. The system also provides a color-coded dashboard, designed to let parents and stakeholders to easily discern performance levels. The color scheme has become a well-known standard for tracking and discussing school performance and it appears to a very effective tool for capturing important performance and organizational measures.

Data about performance are not only frequently used in these districts, they are also very public and transparent. You can easily find interim and summative data on Philadelphia and Denver's websites, and they include portals for parents to monitor the performance of their children and schools.

Though the tools in the districts looked different, they were primarily used in similar ways to monitor and manage performance at all levels and communicate it to the public. Staff in Sacramento, Charlotte-Mecklenburg, Denver, and Long Beach tended to review data together frequently in teams, and interviews in these districts revealed a high level of trust and openness with data and accountability tools and practices.

INFLUENCING FACTORS

Relationships with key stakeholders that deeply impact turnaround work were previously discussed in chapters 2 and 8. The context in which the work happens can either support or completely unravel turnaround efforts. Charlotte-Mecklenburg did not operate under a union contract and thus had more freedom over the things that are most important to utilize: time, people, and money. Relationships with the community seemed positive, and the culture and climate seemed relatively free of conflict. The only concerns mentioned were challenges over budgets and finding a new superintendent. Sacramento and Long Beach are in the same state and thus subject to the same policies; however, Long Beach seemed to have a closer relationship with their union, likely because of the long leadership stability within the distinct. While Sacramento's superintendent, Jonathan Raymond, was relatively new, he did seem to be on the right footing with the union and was able to negotiate protecting teachers who had specialized training for his Priority Schools. Denver had some issues with its union, but they were not voiced in any interviews. The positive factors for Denver are that the state has a positive attitude toward charters and a history of tolerance for trying innovative strategies like DPS's strategic compensation initiative.

The most challenging relationships were found in Philadelphia. The superintendent resigned and left in a flurry of negative publicity, the union had taken the district to court to protect seniority rules, two board members resigned after a public scandal over a charter contract, and many young and new teachers lost their jobs to layoffs. When I asked different people in the district if they thought the turnaround work would be preserved and supported, since it was showing positive outcomes, many were doubtful. With almost a complete inability to control personnel, a vacant superintendency, and two pending new board members, the district is in a great state of flux. If its turnaround work is continued, likely it would be on a much smaller scale, and I doubt it will include many, if any, new charter partners.

On the bright side, outgoing superintendent Arlene Ackerman did have a big influence on a large number of parents, and several leaders in the district and community agree that those parents will continue to pursue a better education for their children using the tips Ackerman provided.

Another obstacle frequently cited was the amount of funds the districts all had to cut from their budgets. Many programs put in place to help make up ground lost by struggling students were cut, teaching forces were reduced, and funds that could be used for recruiting more diverse teachers or to reward or incentivize teachers were lost. While it was a concern for many, most leaders felt that their programs could still continue, only on a smaller scale and/or without any expansion. When asked what they would do when their SIG funds ran out, many leaders were working on sustainability plans and believed that many of the structures seeded by the funds would remain in place.

LESSONS FOR DISTRICTS

While *Bringing School Reform to Scale* was able to provide a detailed list of lessons for districts in areas such as instruction, staffing, and performance management, a similar list on turnarounds from the districts discussed in this book requires more focus on implementation than just the practices themselves. For example, Charlotte-Mecklenburg's human capital strategies were innovative, coherent, and far-reaching, but many could not be easily applied in a district operating under certain types of union contracts. However, almost all districts likely could put into place, even if under contract, succession planning similar to CMS (likely without the use of ranking) to identify and develop their central office talent pool.

The main information gained from this study of five urban districts on turnaround is that it can be driven and scaled at the district level, and that each district offers an area with a particularly innovative or thorough approach. Some lessons from these districts include:

Effective Leaders and Teachers

- Implement strategic succession planning at all levels. Provide ongoing training and apprenticelike opportunities that closely mirror the needs of the position.

- Provide principals with flexibility and closely monitor results. However, consider how freedom with curriculum and program selection can impact alignment across the district and throughout grade levels.

- Provide ample time for leaders and teachers to meet in professional learning communities. Work with staff on how to structure and make effective use of meetings, which should also include the review of data.

- Market turnaround schools to parents, the community, teachers, and principals as a program that is unique and desirable.

- Provide clear guidelines on what is to be taught and learned, and engage staff in frequent collaborative discussions on what mastery looks like in student products.

Curriculum and Instruction

- Institute districtwide strategies that can improve instruction. Make teacher supports, like coaches, easily accessible.

- Increase instructional rigor throughout all grades; ensure that instruction is engaging and focused on college readiness.
- Use formative data to provide frequent feedback on instruction.

Performance Management

- Develop data systems that are easily accessible and produce reports that are simple to interpret and explain. The best systems have one database that includes multiple data sources such as formative and summative assessments, attendance and discipline, grades, and course transcripts.
- Train principals and teachers on how to access and use data on a regular basis to inform instruction.
- Consider how additional monitoring systems can be included in one unifying reporting system like a scorecard. Include student performance information as well as monitoring tools like walk-throughs.
- Build a climate and culture where data is expected to be used to inform decisions and communicate progress.
- Create trust and support around data so that staff members view it as a tool to improve instruction rather than a "gotcha."

Relationships

- Take time to include key stakeholders at the beginning of the planning phase of turnaround or school improvement.
- Engage teacher unions and associations during the entire reform planning process. Negotiate a clause that will

protect teachers who were specifically hired and trained for struggling or turnaround schools from seniority-based layoffs.

- Keep stakeholders updated and informed; communicate with them frequently.
- Emphasize the mission of improving schools for students; show data as often as possible as evidence of positive impact on students.
- Find creative ways to work with parents and community members. Work with them from their current skill and knowledge level, and provide them tips to help them monitor their school and students.

Managing Turnaround

- Consider grouping schools in a cohort that functions like a professional learning community.
- Implement turnaround in feeder patterns if possible.
- Carefully consider the political and cultural aspects of schools when selecting one of the four reform models in SIG. Plan carefully for whatever model is implemented, and communicate it clearly and early to all involved stakeholders.
- Provide ample support for principals implementing any of SIG models; consider moving principals to new schools in teams rather than alone.
- Engage partners as needed and work with them closely to ensure alignment with district and school goals and strategies.
- Find ways to actively communicate and engage with partner CMOs and EMOs, even if they are being implemented as schools separate from the district.

CONCLUSION

The SIG provides significant dollars to states and districts to create the conditions for schools to make dramatic improvement in chronically failing schools. While there is skepticism about certain components of the grant, most agree that it has prompted an important demand and urgency to improve our nation's lowest-performing schools. The windfall of funds will be gone before we know it, but the districts in this book believe they have put structures in place that can sustain the gains they acquired through the grant, and through the infrastructures and effective practices created and indoctrinated. These districts illustrate how turnaround can be successfully implemented from "the trenches" to improve practices and increase achievement across schools. The lessons they provide will continue to inform improvement strategies that we can build on for the future.

NOTES

Introduction

1. L. Pappano, *Inside School Turnarounds* (Cambridge, MA: Harvard Education Press, 2010).

Chapter I

1. R. Flesch Why Johnny Can't Read (New Yowrk: Harper and Row, 1983).
2. Models are described on PowerPoint by the U.S. Department of Education providing an overview of the on School Improvement Grant, www2.ed.gov/programs/sif/090825sigv2.ppt.
3. IES National Center for Education Evaluation and Regional Assistance, *Baseline Analyses of SIG Applications and SIG-Eligible and SIG-Awarded Schools*, NCEE 2011-4019 (Washington, DC: U.S. Department of Education, (May 2011).
4. R. Manwaring, *A Framework for Flexibility for School Turnaround*, May 27, http://www.quickanded.com/2010/05/a-framework-for-flexibility-for-school-turnaround.html.
5. M. Orland, A. Hoffman, and E. S. Vaughn, *Evaluation of the Comprehensive School Reform Program Implementation and Outcomes, 5th-Year Report*, final report prepared for the U.S. Department of Education by WestEd, 2010.
6. J. Knudson, L. Shambaugh, and J. O'Day, *Beyond the School: Exploring a Systemic Approach to School Turnaround*, report by the California Collaborative on District Reform Policy and Practice Brief, February 2011.
7. Manwaring, *A Framework for Flexibility for School Turnaround*.

8. See blog by Thelma Melendez de Sana Ana, Assistant Secretary for Elementary and Secondary Education, http://www.ed.gov/blog/2011/04/supporting-rural-schools/.
9. M. de la Torre and J. Gwynne, *When Schools Close: Effects on Displaced Students in Chicago Public Schools* (Chicago: Consortium on Chicago School Research, 2009).
10. *Baseline Analyses of SIG Applications and SIG-Eligible and SIG-Awarded School.*
11. Orland, Hoffman, and Vaughn, *Evaluation of the Comprehensive School Reform Program Implementation and Outcomes.*
12. See D. Aladjem, B. Birman, M. Orland, J. Harr-Robins, A. Heredia, T. Parrish, and S. Ruffini, *Achieving Dramatic School Improvement: An Exploratory Study*, report prepared for the U.S. Department of Education by WestEd (Washington, DC: U.S. Department of Education, Office of Planning, Evaluation and Policy Development, and Office of Elementary and Secondary Education, 2010).
13. D. Aladjem and K. M. Borman, "Summary of Findings from the National Longitudinal Evaluation of Comprehensive School Reform," paper presented at the 2006 AERA meeting, San Francisco, 2006.
14. W. Togneri and S. E. Anderson, "Beyond Islands of Excellence: What Districts Can Do to Improve Instruction and Achievement in All Schools," 2003, http://www.learningfirst.org/publications/districts/, 11.
15. H. Zavadsky, *Bringing School Reform to Scale: Five Award-Winning Urban Districts* (Cambridge, MA: Harvard Education Press, 2009).
16. J. Kutash, E. Nico, E. Gorin, S. Rahmatullah, and K. Tallant, *The School Turnaround Field Guide* FSG Social Impact Advisors, 2010), http://www.fsg.org/tabid/191/ArticleId/88/Default.aspx?supsh=true.

Chapter 2

1. M. Orland, A. Hoffman, and E. S. Vaughn, *Evaluation of the Comprehensive School Reform Program Implementation and Outcomes, 5th-Year Report*, final report prepared for the U.S. Department of Education by WestEd, 2010.
2. The $1 million Broad Prize, established in 2002, is the largest education award in the country given to school districts. The Broad Prize is awarded each year to honor urban school districts that demonstrate the greatest overall performance and improvement in student achievement while reducing achievement gaps among low-income and minority students.

The Broad Prize has four goals:

- Reward districts that improve achievement levels of disadvantaged students.
- Restore the public's confidence in our nation's public schools by highlighting successful urban districts.
- Create competition and provide incentives for districts to improve.
- Showcase the best practices of successful districts.

For more information, see www.broadprize.org.

3. H. Zavadsky, *Bringing School Reform to Scale: Five Award-Winning Urban Districts* (Cambridge, MA: Harvard Education Press, 2009).
4. Ibid.
5. R Hess, Spinning Wheels: The Politics of Urban School Reform. Brookings Institution Press, Washington D.C.
6. H. Zavadsky, *Bringing School Reform to Scale*; R. Elmore, *School Reform from the Inside Out Policy, Practice, and Performance* (Cambridge, MA: Harvard Education Press, 2004).
7. G. Ratner (with Monty Neill), *Common Elements of Successful School Turnarounds: Research and Experience,* prepared as background for May 19, 2010 House Education and Labor Committee Hearing on "Research and Best Practices on Successful School Turnaround," May 14, 2010.
8. J. Travers and B. Christiansen, *Breaking the Cycle of Failure in Charlotte-Mecklenburg Schools*, report by The Aspen Institute, April 2010.
9. J. Knudson, L. Shambaugh, and J. O'Day, *Beyond the School: Exploring a Systemic Approach to School Turnaround*, report by the California Collaborative on District Reform Policy and Practice Brief, February 2011.

Chapter 3

1. From 2010 Broad Prize data report, http://broadprize.org/asset/1687-nc_charlotte_2011datareport.pdf.
2. A. Helms, "Judge Accuses CMS of 'Academic genocide,'" *Charlotte Observer*, May 24, 2005.
3. Education Resource Strategies, *"Breaking the Cycle of Failure: Strategic Staffing in Charlotte-Mecklenburg Schools*, case study 2009, http://erstrategies.org/resources/details/breaking_the_cycle_of_failure_in_charlotte_schools/.
4. P. Wingert, "An Offer They Wouldn't Refuse: How One District Lured Top Principals to Rescue Its Failing Schools," *Newsweek*, October 18, 2010.
5. CMS Strategic Staffing brochure (fourth in a series of ix).
6. Ibid.

7. CMS board minutes, October 2010, http://www.cms.k12.nc.us/boe/
   Board%20Meeting%20Docs/Minutes-10-12-2010.pdf.
8. The New Teacher Project (TNTP) was created in 1997 by Michelle
   Rhee to provide effective teaches in urban districts. For more information, see http://tntp.org/about-us/our-history.
9. See http://www.datawise-ed.com/DatawiseWebsite/index.php for
   more information.
10. Education Resource Strategies, *Breaking the Cycle of Failure*, p. 13, figure 4.

Chapter 4

1. See school snapshot at district website at www.phila.k12.pa/us/about.
2. T. Bishop, "Pennsylvania Prepares Privatization of Philadelphia Public Schools," World Socialist Website, November 15, 2001, accessed
   10/1/11, http://www.wsws.org/articles/2--1/nov2001/phil-n15.sthml.
3. Presentation by Eve Travers at Friends Association of Higher Education Conference, June 28 2003, https://urbanedjournal.org/achieve/
   Issue4/commentaries.
4. Posted on district website, http://webgui.phila.k12.pa.us/uploads/4C/
   vK/4CvKdh56Cefu-J7JsNIk5A/Philly-2014-results-Sept23.pdf.
5. In Pennsylvania, Corrective Action II is the fifth of five steps for districts not meeting the state's definition of AYP. See http://www.portal.
   state.pa.us/portal/server.pt/community/pennsylvania_accountability_
   system_(pas)/8752/fact_sheet/510191.
6. "Superintendent Arlene C. Ackerman Unveils Plan for Addressing 85
   Under-Performing Schools in the School District of Philadelphia,"
   September 17, 2008, http://www.phila.k12.pa.us/announcements/
   under_performing.html.
7. Forum advertised as "an independent voice for parents, educators, students, and friends of Philadelphia schools. See www.thenotebook.org.

Chapter 5

1. Demographics from 2010 October count. 2011 October count shows
   eighty thousand students; a relatively marked increase for the district.
   See http://communications.dpsk12.org/newsroom/facts.
2. ProComp focuses on teachers' knowledge and skills, provides a comprehensive professional evaluation, uses market incentives for hard-
   to-staff areas, and uses student growth. For more information, see
   http://denverprocomp.dpsk12.org/about/.

3. According to its website, Cambridge Education conducts quality reviews for school improvement processes. DPS spoke highly of this organization. For more information, see http://www.camb-ed-us.com/QualityReviews.aspx.

4. A *mill levy* is the tax rate that is applied to the assessed value of a property. One mill is one dollar per $1,000 dollars of assessed value. It consists of a local portion, which is used to fund area services, and a statewide portion, which is used to fund public schools.

5. See 2010 Denver Plan, http://2010 denverplan.dpsk12.org/pdf/Final2010Denver%Plan.pdf, p. 7.

6. Response to Instruction (RtI) refers to an instructional framework that promotes a well-integrated system connecting general, gifted, supplemental, and special education services in providing high-quality, standards-based instruction and intervention that is matched to students' academic, social-emotional, and behavioral needs. RtI combines core instruction, assessment, and intervention within a multitiered system to increase student achievement and reduce behavior problems. For more information, see http://www.alsde.edu/general/RESPONSE_TO_INSTRUCTION.pdf.

7. Denver Plan, p. 43.

8. Previously, Blueprint did some work with Houston Independent School District. For more information, see http://www.blueprintschools.org.

9. "Union Suit: DPS Abuses Innovation," *Education News Colorado*, http://www.ednewscolorado.org/2011/06/27/20786-lawsuit-dps-abuses-innovation.

10. Denver Plan, p. 32.

Chapter 6

1. See http://www.edsource.org/assets/files/policy/ses/SES_SIG-Issue-paper-plus-enclosure2.pdf.

2. SCUSD Strategic Plan,http://www.scus.edu/administration/documents/2010 Strat Plan.pdf, p. 17.

3. For a good summary description and outline of the process, see http://hepg.org/document/1/.

4. For more information, see R. Elmore and E. City, *Treating the Instructional Core: Education Rounds* (Cambridge, MA: Harvard Education Press, 2009).

5. Quote pulled from one school reflection.

Chapter 7

1. See H. Zavadsky, *Bringing School Reform to Scale: Five Award-Winning Urban Districts* (Cambridge, MA: Harvard Education Press, 2009). The district also had several top high schools in *U.S. News & World Report's* top schools list, was featured in a report by McKinsey & Company in an international comparison, and been featured in several news outlets like NBC's *Today Show*, and CNN's *Headline News*.
2. California awards schools demonstrating exceptional performance, particularly in narrowing achievement gaps, a Distinguished School Award.
3. R. Payne, *A Framework for Understanding Poverty* (Highlands, TX: Aha! Process Inc., 2005). For more information on Ruby Payne, see http://www.ahaprocess.com/About_Us/Ruby_Payne.html.

Chapter 8

1. One of their best-known publications is *The Turnaround Challenge*, http://www.massinsight.org/stg/research/challenge/.
2. Before joining STG, Mike Contompasis had served as the chief operations officer at Boston Public Schools from 1998 to 2005; I interviewed him in that position multiple times.
3. For more information on STG services, see http://www.massinsight.org/stg/services/.
4. For more information, see the Office of School Reform and Innovation website at http://osri.dpsk12.org/dps_charer_compact.
5. D. S. Haas, *An Analysis of Gaps in Funding for Charter Schools and Traditional Districts*, http://www.ipsi.utexas.edu/docs/pubs/brief_05_charter_funding_analysis_v8.pdf.
6. "HISD Loses Four More Principals to KIPP," *School Zone* (blog), *Houston Chronicle*, June 17, 2010, http://blog.chron.com/schoolzone/2010/06/hisd-loses-four-more-principals-to-kipp/.

Chapter 9

1. There are numerous studies on this issue: see, for example, Stacey Childress et al., eds., *Managing School Districts for High Performance: Cases in Public Education Leadership* (Cambridge, MA: Harvard Education Press, 2007); and Robert D. Muller, "The Role of the District in Driving School Reform: A Review for the Denver Commission on Secondary School Reform," http://www.dpsk12.org/pdf/district_role.pdf.
2. See the August 26, 2009, press release at http://www2.ed.gov/news/pressreleases/2009/08262009.html.

ACKNOWLEDGMENTS

The topic of systemic reform has been a passion of mine for a number of years, and it is my goal to bring forward lessons directly from the field to practitioners and others striving to provide a high-quality education to all students. The best way to learn about district and school practices is by spending time speaking to practitioners and looking at schools. This book would not have been possible without the generous time afforded to me by the district leaders, principals, and teachers in the Charlotte-Mecklenburg Schools, School District of Philadelphia, Denver Public Schools, Sacramento City Unified School District, and Long Beach Unified School District. I deeply appreciate your opening your doors to me while preparing for the beginning of a new school year. It was a privilege to meet each of you, and I greatly admire your work and progress. I hope I have represented you well; any errors in this book are strictly my own. Thanks to: Arlene Ackerman, Karen Alexander, Denise Atkinson, Billy Aydlett, Vanessa Benton, Lori Betschel, Tom Boasberg, Emily Buchy, Chuck Carpenter, Curtis Carroll, Felisberto Cedros, Ann Clark, Thomas Darden, Woolworth Davis, Mary DeSplinter, Josh Drake, Francisco Duran, Martina Gomez, Pete Gorman, Rebecca Grant, Laurie

Grosselfinger, Amy Highsmith, Doug Huscher, Larry Irvin, Rahim Islam, Gail Johnson, Rashidah Morgan, Michael Navia, Penny Nixon, Denise "Sparkle" Patterson, Nancy Purcell, Jonathan Raymond, Leticia Rodriguez, Mary Sheldon, Allen Smith, Chris Steinhauser, Timothy Stults, Ron Thompson, William Wade, Laura Wagner, and Debbie Pardo Williams.

Although he just "left" the K–12 practitioner list, I want to thank Steve Adamowski, who has made considerable impact in Harford, for writing the foreword for the book.

Additionally, I thank the leaders of turnaround support organizations who were equally generous with their time: Justin Cohen and Michael Contompasis at School Turnaround Group at Mass Insight; Sandra Elliot and Anna Tilton at Global Partnership Schools; Jennifer Jones; and Rochelle Herring Peniston at Transformation by Design.

I also want to thank Douglas Clayton and the staff at Harvard Education Press for your personalized and patient support, and for encouraging me to bring an idea to fruition. Equally, I'd like to thank Fredrick Hess, the series editor, for always having time to advise me in my work. My gratitude also goes to Amy Dolejs, who provided editing support at ungodly hours.

While this book was written in my "spare time," it was not completed without some time away from my work, so my deep thanks to John Fitzpatrick and George Tang for allowing me the flexibility to conduct site visits.

A special thank you to my husband, Vlad, and my children, Alexander and Benjamin, who were exceedingly patient with long periods of time with no wife or mommy at home.

ABOUT THE AUTHOR

Heather Zavadsky is director of research and implementation for Educate Texas, a unique public-private alliance dedicated to significantly improving the postsecondary readiness of low-income students in Texas. She has more than twenty years of experience in education research and practice, with a particular emphasis on urban education, district data and accountability systems, teacher quality, systemic district and school reform, and special education.

Before coming to Educate Texas, Dr. Zavadsky was the Director of Policy at The University of Texas System Institute for Public School Initiatives. From 2002 to 2006, she managed The Broad Prize for Urban Education for the National Center for Education Accountability, where she led the national data collection and analysis, designed and led a rigorous site visit review process for the finalists, presented the final data to the jury, and showcased the finalist and winning districts through a national symposium, articles, and presentations. She also conducted research for the Charles A. Dana Center and led the charter renewal process for The University of Texas at Austin's University Charter School. Additionally, she taught for six years as a special education teacher and worked extensively with students with autism.

Dr. Zavadsky is the author of *Building School Reform to Scale: Five Exemplary Urban Districts* (Harvard Education Press, 2009), as well as numerous papers and articles in scholarly journals. She holds a bachelor's degree in elementary education, a master's degree in special education, a master's degree in education administration, and a PhD in educational administration with a specialization in educational policy and planning.

INDEX

A Nation at Risk, 5
Achievement Zone (AZ) (CMS), 57–59, 207–208, 215
Ackerman, Arlene, 83, 84, 90, 99, 100, 103, 195–196, 197, 224
Action Walks (Garden Grove), 43
Adequate Yearly Progress (AYP), 6
Advanced Placement (AP), 39
Aldine school district (Texas)
  Broad Prize and, 20
  data use, 41, 42
  instructional approaches, 37
  instructional program selection, 38
  problem-solving process, 45
  raising overall instructional rigor, 39
  stakeholder considerations, 47
  superintendent's role, 25–26, 28
American Institutes of Research (AIR), 10
American Recovery and Reinvestment Act (2009), 7
ASPIRA (Philadelphia), 92
Aspiring Leaders Program, 67, 194

Bill and Melinda Gates Foundation, 69
Bloom's Taxonomy, 37, 39

Blueprint Schools Network, 123, 130–131, 193
Boasberg, Tom, 118, 119, 199
Boston Principal Fellowship, 29
Boston Public Schools (Massachusetts)
  Broad Prize and, 20
  data use, 40, 42
  superintendent's role, 26, 28
Boston Teachers Residency (BTR), 30
Bring School Reform to Scale (*Reform to Scale*), 20, 23
Broad Prize for Urban Education, 19–21, 55, 56, 166, 173

California Collaborative on District Reform (CCDR), 10, 52
California State University Long Beach (CSULB), 173–174
Cambridge Education, 117, 157
Carroll, Curtis, 58
Center for Creative Leadership, 29
Center for Data-Driven Reform in Education, 121
Charlotte-Mecklenburg school district (CMS)
  Achievement Zone, 57–59, 207–208, 215
  background, 55–56

Charlotte-Mecklenburg school
district (CMS), *continued*
challenges and changes, 75–76
climate and culture, 74–75
conclusion, 78–79
curriculum and instruction, 220
district-level reform efforts,
51–52, 194
influencing factors in the reform,
223
leadership as a key element in
turnarounds, 215
organizational structures and
oversight, 207–208
partnerships, 74
performance management using
data, 71–73, 221–222
succession planning (see
succession planning at CMS)
talent management (see Strategic
Staffing Initiative)
turnaround strategy, 3, 57–64
views from the schools, 76–78
charter management organizations
(CMOs). *See also* external-
partner-led reform
advantages and disadvantages of,
199–200
in Denver schools, 119–120,
198–200
versus non-charter schools, 94–95
in Philadelphia schools, 195–198
Renaissance Schools in Philadelphia, 50, 88, 91–95, 212
results, 93–94
strategies, 93
chief academic officer (CAO) (CMS),
62

CMOs. *See* charter management
organizations
CMS. *See* Charlotte-Mecklenburg
school district
coaching model, 32
Coalition to Keep Our Public
Schools Public (Philadelphia),
83
Cohen, Carl, 27, 166, 184
Cohen, Justin, 188
Collegiate Prep Academy (CPA)
(DPS), 133–134
compensation
based on teacher evaluations, 70
charter versus noncharter schools,
197
financial incentives at CMS, 60, 61
ProComp at DPS, 124
Comprehensive Accountability Plan
(Norfolk), 43
Comprehensive School Reform
(CSR), 6–7, 14–15
Contompasis, Mike, 188
CSR Demonstration Program, 10
CSULB (California State University
Long Beach), 173–174
culturally responsive curriculum,
153
curriculum and instruction
benefits of setting at the district
level, 35–36
Charlotte-Mecklenburg, 220
curriculum defined, 37
Denver, 126–127, 220
fundamental needs determina-
tion, 34–35
Long Beach, 174–175, 219
Philadelphia, 97

program selection practices,
37–38
raising overall instructional rigor,
38–39
Sacramento, 152–154, 219
school turnaround role, 36–37

Data Inquiry process, 148–150, 154,
191
data systems
as a driver for improving district
practices, 40–41
issues impacting SIGs and, 50
learning objectives monitoring,
41–42
for performance management,
71–73, 221–222
for refining instruction, 221
tools, practices, and culture
considerations, 40
transparency of data, 43–44
trust and, 44
tying data to district and school
goals, 42–43
Data Wise, 73, 147
Denver Classroom Teachers
Association (DCTA), 124
Denver Public Schools (DPS)
allocation of SIG funds, 120–121
background, 113–114
challenges and changes, 131–132
charter schools relationship,
119–120, 198–200
choice and community
engagement facet, 118–119
climate and culture, 128–130
communications plan, 122
community outreach, 128–130

conclusion, 139–140
curriculum and instruction,
126–127, 220
external-partner-led reform, 193
Greenlee's turnaround, 137
human capital strategies,
123–125
indicators used in SPF, 116
influencing factors in the reform,
223
innovation status meaning, 120
Lake International's turnaround,
138–139
Montbello's efforts to transform,
132–137
organizational structures and
oversight, 209–211
partnerships, 123, 130–131
performance framework, 116, 117t
performance management,
124–125, 127, 222
plan levers, 118
preliminary work, 114
process initiation, 117–118
regional application, 121–122
team effort approach, 122–123
theory of action, 114–115
turnaround strategy, 3, 114–123
unions and, 217
view from schools, 132–139
Denver Summit School Network
(DSSN), 122, 210
District-Charter Collaboration
Contract (DPS), 198
district-level reform
Broad Prize and, 19–21
centralized versus decentralized
reform, 178–179, 203–204

district-level reform, *continued*
  Charlotte-Mecklenburg approach,
    51–52, 194
  charter school partnerships
    (see charter management
    organizations)
  cohort model use, 213
  compared to external-partner-led
    reform (see external-partner-
    led reform)
  crucial reform areas, 51–52
  curriculum and instruction,
    34–39, 218–221
  curriculum and instruction
    lessons, 225–226
  data use (see data systems)
  human capital turnaround
    strategies, 214–218
  influencing factors, 47–48,
    222–224
  instructional alignment
    importance, 204–205
  interconnectiveness of school
    improvement elements,
    21–23
  intervention and adjustment,
    44–47
  leaders and teachers effectiveness
    and, 225
  Long Beach's approach, 194–195
  main considerations, 212–213
  organizational structures and
    oversight turnaround
    strategies, 207–212
  performance management
    lessons, 226
  policy role, 48–51
  recognition of need for alignment
    around core elements, 23
  relationships lessons, 226–227
  SIG's role in, 206, 228
  superintendent's leadership
    importance, 25–30, 213
  turnaround management lessons,
    227
DOE (U.S. Department of
  Education), 7, 9, 10
DPS. *See* Denver Public Schools
DSSN (Denver Summit School
  Network), 122, 210
Duncan, Arne, 7, 205
Duran, Francisco, 102

Edison Schools, 83
educational management
  organization (EMO), 50
Education Resource Strategies (ERS)
  (CMS), 67, 77
Effective School Leaders programs
  (CMS), 67
Elementary and Secondary
  Education Act (ESEA), 6
Elmore, Richard, 152–153, 218
EMO (educational management
  organization), 50
Empowering Excellent Educators
  (DPS), 124
Empowerment School Response
  (ESR) teams (Philadelphia), 88,
  210–211
ESEA (Elementary and Secondary
  Education Act), 6
Essential Elements of Effective
  Instruction, 37, 39

external-partner-led reform. *See also* charter management organizations
basis of decision to engage, 200–202, 213–214
conclusion, 202
Denver Public Schools, 193
embedding the strategies of, 192
lead partner model, 189–190
leveraging, 192
Mass Insight Education, 188–190
obstacles holding districts back, 189
organic process characterized by Data Inquiry, 191
performance management, 221–222
in Sacramento, 190–192
situation when needed, 192

Far Northeast (FNE) region (DPS), 121, 210
Finding Opportunities; Creating Un-paralleled Success (FOCUS), 58
focus schools, 45
freedom and flexibility with account-ability (FFA) (CMS), 72–73
Fryer, Roland Jr., 130–131

Garden Grove school district (California)
Broad Prize and, 20
data use, 43–44
intervention techniques, 45
raising overall instructional rigor, 39
superintendent's role, 26, 28

Gorman, Peter, 28, 56, 71, 72, 75–76, 194
Green Beret principals (Philadelphia), 215–216
Greenlee Elementary (DPS), 137

Herring-Peniston, Rochelle, 147, 148, 157, 190–192
Hornbeck, David, 82
Houston schools, 200
Hughes, Robert, 17
human capital strategies
Denver, 123–125
department practices and, 32–34
emergence as a major focus, 218
fundamental importance of, 214
leadership as a key element, 215–216
leadership stability as a major factor, 27–29
Philadelphia, 95–96
professional development importance, 29–30
Sacramento, 151–152
superintendent leadership examples, 25–27
talent management importance, 24–25, 29
teachers and, 30–31, 216–218
training and support, 31–32

Innovation Schools Act (2008, Colorado), 120
instructional coaches, 32
Instructional Non-Negotiables, 37, 39
International Baccalaureate Programme (IB), 138

Investing in Innovation (i3) funds, 8
Irvin, Larry, 133, 135
Islam, Rahim, 93, 197–198

Knowledge is Power Program (KIPP), 200
Kujawa, Nadine, 25–26

Lake International (DPS), 138–139
Leaders for Tomorrow (CMS), 67
leadership
    as a key element in turnarounds, 215–216
    superintendents' role, 25–29
    training in (see talent management)
Leadership and Capacity Development Department (LCD) (Norfolk), 32
Leadership and Investment For Transformation (Project L.I.F.T.), 59
Leadership Institute (Boston), 29
Leading Effective Academic Practice (LEAP) (DPS), 124
Long Beach Unified School District (Long Beach), 27
    background, 165–166
    basis of success, 166–168
    Broad Prize and, 20
    challenges and changes, 178–179
    climate and culture, 177
    collaborative approach, 168
    conclusion, 185
    curriculum and instruction, 174–175, 219
    district-level reform, 194–195

human capital strategies, 172–174, 217
influencing factors in the reform, 223
instructional approaches, 37
intervention techniques, 45
organizational structures and oversight, 208–209
partnerships, 173–174, 177–178
perceptions of SIG and the turnaround, 180
performance management, 175–176
pilot school approach, 171–172
raising overall instructional rigor, 39
sixth-grade academy model, 168–171
superintendent's longevity, 28
turnaround strategy, 3, 168–172
view from schools, 181–185

Manning, Howard, 56, 60
Manwaring, Rob, 10
Marshall Academy of the Arts (Long Beach), 181–183
Mary Butler Visual & Performing Arts Magnet (Long Beach), 183–185
Mass Insight Education, 188–190
Mastery Charter Schools (Philadelphia), 92
Measuring Effective Teachers (MET), 69, 125, 220
Montbello High School (DPS), 132–137
Mosaica Education (Philadelphia), 92
MyBPS (Boston), 40

New Leaders for New Schools, 67, 194

New Teacher Project (CMS), 216

No Child Left Behind (NCLB, 2002), 6–7

Norfolk school district (Virginia), 27
  Broad Prize and, 20
  centralized versus decentralized reform, 205
  data use, 42, 43
  instructional approaches, 37
  raising overall instructional rigor, 39
  superintendent's longevity and, 28

Office of Choice and Enrollment Services (OCES) (DPS), 119

Office of Community Engagement (DPS), 128

Office of Parent Engagement (DPS), 128

Office of School Reform and Innovation (DPS), 198

outcome-based education, 5

parents
  importance of in the turnaround strategy, 100
  relationship with schools and districts, 47–48
  services that draw parents in, 101
  successful outreach to, 102–103

partnerships. *See* charter management organizations; external-partner-led reform

Payne, Ruby, 184

Payzant, Tom, 26, 47, 204

performance management. *See also* talent management
  Charlotte-Mecklenburg's data focus, 71–73, 221–222
  Denver, 124–125, 127, 222
  Philadelphia, 97–98

Philadelphia, School District of
  attention paid to the culture, 108–109
  attention paid to the students, 110
  background, 81–84
  changes and challenges, 104–106
  charter schools relationship, 99–100, 200
  climate and culture, 98–99
  comprehensive alignment focus, 87
  conclusion, 111
  curriculum and instruction, 97
  district goals, 84
  hiring of Wade, 106
  human capital strategies, 95–96
  influencing factors in the reform, 223–224
  instructional approach attention, 107–108
  intervention plan for Empowerment schools, 87–89
  leadership as a key element in turnarounds, 215
  organizational structures and oversight, 211–212
  parent/district relationship, 100–104
  performance management, 97–98
  per-pupil funding, 82

Philadelphia, School District of,
    continued
    Promise Academies innovation
        model, 89–91
    Renaissance Schools, 50, 88,
        91–95, 212
    results, 110–111
    school/community connection
        efforts, 109
    situation assessment, 106–107
    talent management attention, 107
    turnaround plan elements, 85–87
    turnaround strategy, 3, 84–85
    unions and, 217
    view from schools, 106–111
PLCs. *See* professional learning
    communities
Principal Leadership Development
    (CMS), 67
principals
    Charlotte-Mecklenburg, view of
        reforms in, 76–78
    Denver, view of reforms in,
        132–139
    leadership as a key element in
        turnarounds, 215–216
    Long Beach, view of reforms in,
        181–185
    Philadelphia, view of reforms in,
        106–111
    professional development at CMS,
        67–68
    replacing under SIG program, 10
    Sacramento, view of reforms in,
        159–161
Priority Schools. *See* Sacramento
    City Unified School District

ProComp at DPS, 124, 217
professional development
    at DPS, 125
    importance of, 29–30
    programs for teacher training and
        hiring, 30–31
    training and support, 31–32
professional learning communities
    (PLCs)
    Charlotte-Mecklenburg school
        district, 207–208
    at Long Beach, 168, 172
    Sacramento City Unified School
        District, 208
    SIG funding for, 121
Project L.I.F.T. (Leadership
    and Investment For
    Transformation), 59
Promise Academies (Philadelphia),
    88, 89–91, 105, 212
Promise Neighborhood Schools
    (Philadelphia), 90–91
Pughsley, James, 56

Race to the Top, 7–8
Raymond, Jonathan, 142, 150, 190
Renaissance schools (Philadelphia),
    50, 88, 91–95, 212
Restart model, 8, 50
root cause analysis, 45

Sacramento City Unified School
    District (SCUSD)
    background, 141–143
    central office structures creation,
        143
    challenges and changes, 157–159

climate and culture, 156–157

conclusion, 162–163

curriculum and instruction,
152–154, 219

Data Inquiry process, 148–150

Data Wise and, 147

domains affecting the overall
quality of a school, 154

external-partner-led reform,
190–192

human capital strategies, 151–152,
217

influencing factors in the reform,
223

information gained from data
inquiry reports, 161–162

instructional strategies and
principles, 152–153

organizational structures and
oversight, 208–209

parental and community
engagement, 156–157

partnerships, 147, 157

perceptions of SIG and the
turnaround, 158–159

performance management,
154–156, 222

pillars of, 144–145

plan design process, 147

Priority Schools, 145–146

turnaround strategy, 3,
143–150

view from schools, 159–161

year one progress, 150

year one roll out, 149

School Advisory Council (SAC)
(Philadelphia), 92

School Boards

choice of superintendent and,
28–29

as an influencing factor in reform,
47, 51

issues impacting SIGs and, 51

state takeover in Philadelphia, 82

School Improvement Grant (SIG)

about, 7

centralization versus
decentralization debate, 16,
203–204

criticisms of, 9–13

CSR results to date, 14–15

districts' role in turnarounds,
15–17

DOE work on addressing
challenges, 12

essential elements of school
improvement, 2–3

establishment of, 7–8

factors affecting districts' ability
to follow requirements of,
49–51

funds distribution guidelines, 8–9

good done by, 48, 228

intervention models, 8, 10–12

meaning of turnaround, 13–14

perceptions of at Long Beach, 180

perceptions of at Sacramento,
158–159

purpose and operation, 206

role in district-level reform, 206,
228

school closure model, 8

tiers, 9

turnaround defined, 4

School Improvement Plans (CMS),
71–72
School Loop (Long Beach), 176
School Performance Framework
(SPF) (DPS), 116
School Progress Reports (CMS), 71
school quality review (SQR)
(SCUSD), 154
School Quality Reviews (SQR)
(CMS), 71
school reform and turnaround
essential elements of school
improvement, 2–3
federal role in (see School
Improvement Grant)
past efforts, 5–7
strategies for (see individual
school districts)
turnaround defined, 4, 5
School Reform Commission (SRC)
(Philadelphia), 82
School Turnaround Group (STG),
188–190
Schwalm, Laura, 26, 28, 43
Shelton, Mary, 150, 158
SIG. See School Improvement Grant
Simpson, John, 27, 42, 205
Single School Plan (Garden Grove),
43
Smith, Allen, 122–123, 131, 132
Spinning Wheels (Hess), 22
SSI. See Strategic Staffing Initiative
(CMS)
Steinhauser, Chris, 27, 166, 168, 178,
184
Strategic Plan 2014 (Philadelphia),
84

Strategic Staffing Initiative (SSI)
(CMS)
communications plan, 61–62
financial incentives, 60, 61
goal of, 52, 59–60
results, 62, 63–64f
strategy used to attract strong
principals, 60–61
team staffing, 61
Street, John F., 82
Success for All, 15
succession planning at CMS
new staff hiring, 68–69
organizational levels addressed, 65
pipeline development process, 66
professional development
opportunities, 67
system-wide approach, 65
talent identification process,
66–68
teacher evaluations, 69–70
superintendents
crucial role in schools' success,
25–30, 213
strategies used by (see individual
school districts)

talent management. See also
performance management
at DPS, 123–125
human resources department
practices and, 32–34
in Philadelphia schools, 96
principals' preference for selecting
teachers, 173
at Sacramento, 151
strategy used at CMS, 52, 59–64